MARY GORDON DUFFEE'S

SKETCHES OF ALABAMA

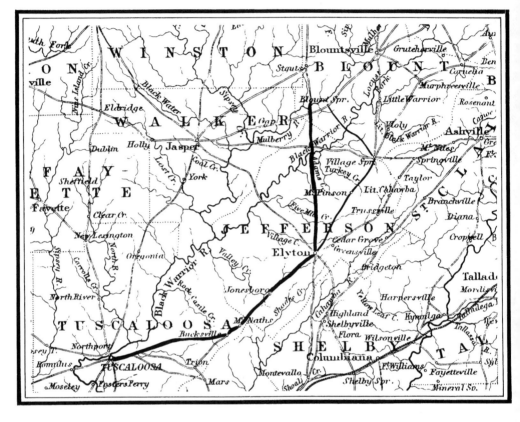

This section from Bartholomew's Alabama map of 1856 shows the stage road on which Mary Gordon Duffee traveled from Tuscaloosa through Elyton, crossroads of travel, to Blount Springs.

MARY GORDON DUFFEE'S
SKETCHES OF ALABAMA

*Being an Account of the Journey
from Tuscaloosa to Blount Springs
through Jefferson County
on the old Stage Roads*

NOW FIRST PUBLISHED IN BOOK FORM
PREPARED FOR THE PRESS WITH INTRODUCTION AND NOTES
BY VIRGINIA POUNDS BROWN AND JANE PORTER NABERS

Illustrated with advertisements from the *Jones Valley
Times* of 1854

THE UNIVERSITY OF ALABAMA PRESS

The five articles in this book were first published
in *The Alabama Review*, Vol. VI (1953) No. 4,
Vol. IX (1956) Nos. 2, 3, and 4, and Vol. X (1957)
No. 1, copyrighted, 1953, 1956, 1957, by The
University of Alabama Press.

For *Margaret Miller*
and
Enid Bodine Winston

Contents

EDITORS' NOTE

Sketches of Alabama by Mary Gordon Duffee originally appeared as fifty-nine articles in the Birmingham *Weekly Iron Age* from 1885 through 1887. Editor Charles Hayes, in financial difficulty, solicited Miss Duffee, a personal friend, for the exclusive rights to publish the articles. "To help him," she says, "and with a view to future profits from its sale, I let him have the exclusive right to publish the *Sketches* in this State, reserving all rights to ownership of the articles. All I asked him to pay me was twenty (20) subscriptions to the paper as long as I wrote said *Sketches*. This he did. My writing brought much money to the paper, but not one dollar came to me." The *Sketches*, however, did not solve Hayes' financial problems; in 1887 he sold out to the *Age Herald* and no more *Sketches* appeared.

Twenty-two years later, a woman of sixty-four, Miss Duffee began frustrating attempts to get the *Sketches* published in book form. Her correspondence in 1908 with Thomas M. Owen, Director of the Alabama State Department of Archives and History, reveals Dr. Owen's intent to have the *Sketches* published. He wrote her that he would "not be content until we have your *Sketches* in print. They will constitute one of the most interesting chapters in the history and growth of the state." Unfortunately, neither Miss Duffee nor the Department had a complete file of the *Sketches* at that time, and the missing numbers could not be located while plans for publication were still active. Subsequently the Department completed its file of the *Iron Age,* and in 1937, as a W.P.A. Writer's Project, the *Sketches* were typed from the newspaper file and placed in the Manuscript Room of the Department. Under the direction of the Birmingham Library Board another copy was typed by the W.P.A. for the Southern Collection of the Birmingham Public Library.

Mary Gordon Duffee has rendered in the *Sketches* an immeasurable service to the historical literature of Alabama. Proof of this lies in their extensive use as source material by every competent writer on Jefferson County and Birmingham. Ethel Armes acknowledges her indebtedness to Miss Duffee for much of the material in the first chapters of her exhaustive book, *The Story of Coal and Iron in Alabama.* The early histories of Jefferson County are so permeated with the *Sketches* that it is difficult to separate the authors from their source.

Regrettably Mary Gordon Duffee's style in the *Sketches* hampers their use both as historical material and for general reading. She wrote in the ornate, wordy language of the Victorian era, and scattered lines of poetry, sometimes her own, confuse the text. Biographical material is frequently buried in eulogies in which she may digress for pages. In spite of these obvious literary faults, Miss Duffee wrote entertainingly and with a dedication to Alabama, particularly to Jones Valley, that distinguishes her work.

The editors, concurring with earlier historians and writers as to the historical value of the *Sketches,* felt that, if properly prepared, the *Sketches* would also make a delightful book for the general reader. Toward that end we have rewritten and revised the *Sketches* by curtailing the wordiness, omitting lengthy digressions, and placing the contents in a logical arrangement. We have employed advertisements from a local newspaper contemporary with the period to add interest and flavor to the text. We have been careful to preserve the historical value of the *Sketches* and to verify their contents with footnotes which we have supplemented with additional information on Jefferson County history.

Introductory Essay

Mary Gordon Duffee
Historian of the Hill Country.

In 1859,[1] when John T. Milner recommended building the
Alabama Central Railroad through the state's hill country,[2]
Senator Walker of Calhoun County took the legislative floor
and, contemptuously slapping Milner's report on the desk,
said, "That country up there is so poor that a buzzard would
have to carry provisions on his back or starve to death on his
passage."[3]

The Alabama hill country had its champions, however, but,
strange to say, they were not the landowners who scratched the
iron ore as they plowed the fields. Rather, they were travelers
who, passing through Jones Valley over the years, noticed the
outcroppings of coal and iron ore. For instance, in the 1830's
young Frank Gilmer, as he crossed over Red Mountain, was
puzzled by the red dust on his horse's hoofs. Curious, he dismounted, examined the purplish rocks, and slipped specimens
into his saddle-bag. Later, in Montgomery, he made a fortune in the mercantile business, but he never forgot the iron
ore buried in the hill country.

Two decades later, largely because of Frank Gilmer's efforts, John T. Milner's railroad recommendation was ap-
proved by the Alabama legislature. Then came geologists
from as far away as England to study and report on the unusual concentration of mineral wealth in this undeveloped section of Alabama.[4]

Inconspicuous among this group of travelers through Jones
Valley was a young girl from Tuscaloosa, Mary Gordon

Duffee. Her father, Matthew Duffee, born in Ireland, had come in 1823 to Tuscaloosa. There he became the genial proprietor of the Washington House, the most elaborate and popular tavern in the capital, where legislators and university men gathered to discuss politics of the day.[5]

A decade or more before the Civil War Duffee purchased the resort hotel at Blount Springs known as the Goffe House, renamed it the Duffee House, and operated it successfully until 1869, when it was destroyed by fire.[6] Duffee's persuasive advertisements of the "best watering place of the Southern Country" at Blount Springs appeared in the *Jones Valley Times* (Elyton) in the 1850's. Special passenger hacks left Elyton three times a week; the fare was four dollars and the boarding rate at the hotel one dollar a day.[7]

In the spring of each year Matthew Duffee packed up his family and servants in Tuscaloosa, loaded them in a carriage and wagons, and set out on the four-day journey up Jones Valley to Blount Springs for the summer season. The first vehicle in the caravan was the family carriage in which Mary Gordon Duffee rode with her mother and three older brothers. While only six years old in 1850,[8] Mary Gordon grew to cherish the familiar journey to and from Blount Springs. The pioneer families whom she met along the route and the landmarks which she learned to recognize fired her imagination. She became avidly interested in the struggles that had made the valley an agrarian community and in the vision of mineral wealth that would transform it into an industrial empire.

Many years later Mary Gordon Duffee recalled every mile of those journeys for her *Sketches of Alabama* which appeared as fifty-nine separate articles in the Birmingham *Weekly Iron Age* in 1886 and 1887.[9] Using as a framework for the *Sketches* these annual childhood treks, she wove together multitudinous details of fact and lore concerning the history and people of the hill country from Indian occupation to the founding of Birmingham. She described the trip on the old Huntsville Road from Tuscaloosa to Jonesboro and Elyton, on to Roebuck's, and then across the less traveled route to Blount Springs. On this geographical frame-work she superimposed

BLOUNT SPRINGS,
Blount County, Ala.

THIS delightful Watering Place is now open for the present season, by M. DUFFEE, who is there in readiness to receive a large number of guests in expectation of keeping the Springs this season. He has used all diligence in his garden arrangements, as well as other necessary appendages notwithstanding *Jack Frost's* victory over the Peach crop, there is plenty of the most delicious kind to be had from the neighboring mountains.

It is hardly necessary to enumerate the great and healing qualities of these waters. There are nine distinct Springs, generally used including Red Sulpher from No 1 to 5; White Sulpher, No. 1, 2; Sweet and Black Sulpher, and the celebrated Hepatic. all these Springs invigorate and produce healthfulness, and patrons will be greatly benefitted by their healing qualities if they stay long enough to give them a fair trial.

Good Music will be at the Springs.

A Tri-weekly mail from Elyton to th Springs is carried in a fine new Passenge. Hack, which will run regularly three times a week from the 10th of July until the first of October,—carrying the mail and passengers Time of leaving Elyton, every Tuesday, Thursday, and Saturday mornings, and will arrive at the Springs same day. Fare from Elyton to the Springs $4. As the owners of the hack line drive themselves, the greatest care and attention to passengers will be observed: a good dinner house will be selected, where ample time will be given passengers to rest.

There is at the Springs a sufficient quantity of old corn and other provender, to feed the horses of all guests that may visit the Springs.

RATES OF BOARD.

Guests over 10 years old, per day,	$1 00
Children over 2 and under 10 years, p. d.	50
Servants,	50
Horses,	50

The above will be the rates of board for all time over ten days, under ten days will be charged at transient rates. M. DUFFEE.

July 1, 1854. 16tf.

From the Jones Valley Times,
August 31, 1854

biographical dissertations on the pioneer families and their descendants, historical details of Indian wars, pioneer settlement, growth of schools and churches, development of railroads and mineral wealth, and descriptions of minutiae of daily life, farming practices, and local customs.

Thomas M. Owen, founder of the Alabama State Department of Archives and History, once remarked that Mary Gordon Duffee knew more Alabama history than anyone else in the state.[10] In fact, Dr. Owen wrote her in 1908 that he would "not be content until we have your *Sketches* in print. They will constitute one of the most interesting chapters in the history and growth of the state."[11]

The *Sketches* are written in the florid, verbose language of the Victorian era. Particularly in the biographical material do eulogistic digressions veil the pertinent matter. The extensive use of the *Sketches*, however, as source material for early Alabama historical research proves their value.[12]

The history of Alabama's hill country emphasizes primarily the dramatic story of coal grubbed out of river banks, iron ore dug on Red Mountain, and a determined group of men fighting against great odds to market these natural resources. Mary Gordon Duffee epitomized this development when she expressed the intent of the *Sketches* thus:

Historian, do I style myself! No, rather the traveler weaving a narrative of Jones Valley as I first beheld it before its quiet beauty gave way to the smoke of furnace and engine. Let me view again the roads I traveled from my Tuscaloosa home to Blount Springs. Let me greet again the men and women of that Valley who believed so faithfully in its future that I cannot recall a single hour spent with them in which the store of minerals of the hill country was not the essence and point.[13]

She tells in one of the *Sketches* that her delight even as a child was to leave the family carriage and ride ahead with a man named Timmons who answered her questions about the bluffs of red rock and the coal exposed here and there.[14] Elsewhere she records in detail David Hanby's coal operation on the Warrior River:

During the summer and autumn Hanby gave employment to a large force of men in getting out coal. He had no difficulty in obtaining ample help, since labor was cheap and plentiful. The coal was mined partly on the ridges, from which wagons hauled it to the landing place, and partly on the steep sides of the river, where it could be shovelled into flatboats moored below.

These huge flatboats were made of immense slabs of timber carefully selected for soundness and strength, hewn to the proper dimensions, and seasoned thoroughly. These slabs were hauled to the banks, laid in parallel lines, and a strong floor of rough-hewn boards called puncheons was laid between them and securely fastened so as to resist all shocks of driftwood and projecting rocks. The floor was caulked with melted tar to render it waterproof. Part of the boat was covered in order to protect the men, who cooked their own provisions and slept aboard. A rude helm was constructed by placing a piece of grooved timber at one end; then by the aid of a long pole, the pilot steered his primitive craft, while men with oars were ready at the side to assist him when necessary.

At the first rise in the river the boats loaded with coal were floated down the Warrior. At night, if the current was deep and the moon shone, they floated on, but, if there were clouds and a heavy fog, the men pulled to the banks, tied up their boats, and remained in safety until daylight. The dangers were many, especially at the Squaw Shoals above Tuscaloosa, which were so rocky and rapid as to imperil the lives of the boatmen and require the display of great nerve and skill on the part of the pilot.[15] Sometimes in spite of every precaution the boat was wrecked on the treacherous shoals, and the entire cargo lost, the crew barely escaping with their lives.

At Mobile the lumber in the boats was sold for firewood,[16] and the crew was promptly paid and discharged. There the coal found a ready market at remunerative price because of its well-known good quality and the popularity of Mr. Hanby.[17]

Of equal importance with this account of pioneer coal operation is Mary Gordon Duffee's description of early ore mining. She recalls her first glimpse of iron ore exposed at Dick Murphy's, between Tuscaloosa and Elyton, in these words: "In Tuscaloosa Murphy bought his plows made of English iron to use against the rocks of iron ore in his own fields. His old face showed surprise when my father asked him why he didn't reduce the ores, and the next moment he smiled as he told us he couldn't, 'but it was a dead sure thing to be done someday.' "[18]

In this vicinity was located the Tannehill furnace, the history of which Mary Gordon Duffee traces from its inception to its destruction by Federal troops during the Civil War.[19] Of the Oxmoor furnace in Jefferson County, destroyed by the same raiders, she gives this first hand account:

During March I had passed through Oxmoor, peaceful and hospitable. On the afternoon of April 13 I gazed upon a scene of ruin at this same spot that makes me shudder now as I recall it. It was in Montevallo when the invading army entered. All of my brothers were at the front, my parents at Blount Springs, sixty-five miles away. About sunset rolling drums and prancing horses in a long column approached Montevallo. All night we waited, knowing a battle was imminent as the forces of Forrest and Roddey were on the southern outskirts. Firing began at the depot and a heavy skirmish ensued. Two days afterward, Miss Emmie Bailey and I organized a band of women and children to go down the railroad to Brierfield to search for the wounded and dying.

Then I resolved to make my way home by foot. I met starvation on every hand and was grateful for the hominy and buttermilk graciously shared with me. After a walk of thirty miles, I reached Oxmoor at the close of a tenderly beautiful day of early spring. There I hoped to receive food and shelter to relieve my hunger and fatigue. As I neared the familiar scene, my heart sank at the strange stillness of the landscape. Here and there a broken-down army horse searched for tender young grass. Wild blue flags and wild honeysuckle bloomed among the rocks. The tranquillity was overwhelmingly lonely.

At last I mustered courage to venture on and found myself standing by blackened ruins, against the wall of the furnace tower. As I contemplated the silent houses up the hill, the deserted road, the awful truth flashed upon me in despair. In bitter despair, blinded with tears, I knelt and prayed.

Rising, I saw smoke issuing from a chimney at the summit of a high hill. Wearily I climbed the steep and rugged path to this sign of security. I did not presume to ask for food, only a sleeping place on the floor. The kind head of the family was a son-in-law of old man Moses Stroup, the pioneer iron-maker. He and his family welcomed me graciously and shared with me what little they had.

Refreshed by a night of unbroken sleep, I bade these blessed friends adieu at an early hour and wended my solitary way to the wretched ruins. The morning sun shone from a cloudless sky, and I lingered long amid those mournful scenes, then pursued my journey up the road, past the silent homes, only one or two of which were left to greet me. On the summit I stopped to view the grave of a child of Mr. Haynes, a scientist. To my horror a wayfarer told me that stragglers from the army had broken the marble stones and dug into the grave in search of treasure. I hurried away. . .

The following morning through a lane of mud and water I made my way to Elyton. But ere I retired that night I knelt and dedicated my future life to the glory of my native state.[20]

Linked inevitably with the development of the Jones Valley mineral lands was an adequate system of transportation. Mary Gordon Duffee realized this and devoted several of the *Sketches* to railroad history. In 1854 she watched with childish interest the breaking of ground in Tuscaloosa for the beginning of the Northeast & Southwest Railroad.[21] Later, as a young woman just before the Civil War, she witnessed at her father's hotel at Blount Springs a subscription barbecue held to forward the cause of the South & North Alabama Railroad.[22] After the conflict, in 1866, she looked back on the ruins of the South and North Alabama in Jefferson County and wrote, "Briers grew over the gradings, bridges were decaying and falling to pieces. The once lively camp of Engineer Boyle could be discovered only by the charred remains of horseshoes and iron ties of an old cart wheel."[23]

Finally, after many vicissitudes, the South & North Alabama Railroad was rebuilt and opened for business on October 1, 1872, thus insuring the founding of Birmingham, whose very existence depended on the successful transportation of coal and iron to world markets.[24] To one so keenly concerned with every phase of industrial development the birth of this great workshop town was a subject of enthusiastic interest. For help in telling the story Mary Gordon Duffee turned to the several founders of Birmingham, but chiefly to James R. Powell, whom she had known since childhood as her father's friend. It was Powell who selected her to give the welcoming address to the New York Press Association in Birmingham in 1873,[25] and it was he who summoned her from her newspaper work in New York, suggesting Birmingham as a fitting subject for her journalistic efforts. She returned to devote herself to writing about the growing town and about Powell himself who styled her "the historian of my life."[26] When the financial panic and the cholera epidemic apparently had bankrupted Birmingham, Powell retired to his Mississippi plantation in 1874, and Mary Gordon Duffee returned to Blount Springs, where, since the destruction of the hotel by fire, her family had lived atop

Duffee's Mountain. Here she stayed for the remaining forty-five years of her life, devoting her time and enthusiasm to study and writing.

The *Sketches of Alabama, Jones Valley* constitute the main literary work of Mary Gordon Duffee. In addition to these she produced a literary potpourri. Occasionally using the pseudonym, Mary Duff Gordon, and often writing anonymously, she contributed articles on Southern industries and industrial leaders to *The South*, a New York newspaper.[27] She wrote for the New York *Weekly Tribune*, Leslie's publications, and the *Youth's Companion*, for which she also solicited subscriptions.[28] She compiled several guide books describing the route of Southern railroads.[29] When she accepted the invitation of the Louisville & Nashville Railroad to write a guide book on Mammoth Cave, she was provided a private car.[30] She recalls in the *Sketches*:

I spent nearly every day of the month of June, 1875, in the avenues and grottoes of Mammoth Cave, Kentucky. I well remember one sunny morning when a large party of us ventured as far as Croghan's Hall, the terminus of Mammoth Cave nine miles from the mouth. During the day clouds arose, and a terrific flood of rain fell, causing a rise in the streams of the cave. We, of course, knew nothing of this storm while returning across Echo River, a stream usually fifty feet deep, very wide and clear as crystal, but, as we approached our landing, we failed to observe the usual light. Our faithful guides, old Matt Nicholas and William, sprang into the stream and pulled the boat with ropes while we lay down full length with the shallow boat fast filling with water. The low archway, four feet high in dry season, scraped our backs for thirty feet. We were thankful indeed when we crawled out and found ourselves in the lofty sand-covered floor of River Avenue. Ten o'clock that night when we were safe on the surface of the earth, all the clouds had passed away, and the skies were luminous with stars.[31]

Mary Gordon Duffee's need for remunerative work is revealed in her private correspondence, which indicates that she even wrote advertising copy in the form of testimonials for patent medicine companies. Evidently, her best account was the Pacific Borax Company, which she endorsed in 1905, for in 1910 she was still using their stationery. On it is imprinted their letterhead showing a picture of "20 Mule Team hauling

Borax out of Death Valley" under which is printed a seventy-six line dissertation signed by Mary Gordon Duffee. Of Borax she wrote: "From the bathroom, laundry, kitchen and sick room to the quarantine camp, from the noxious germ-sewer to the demands of fashion and the charms of beauty it is the one article to be depended upon. No home, business office, or railroad employee should be without it. . . In the cause of humanity, of timely help to the noble physicians who risk their lives for us and those who guard the line; in behalf of help to those who toil that their labors may be made lighter and their homes free from danger, I ask a fair trial of '20 Mule Team' borax."[32]

Mary Gordon Duffee's verses earned her the title "poetess of the mountain." Many of the *Sketches* are introduced with an original verse, and J. W. DuBose's *Mineral Wealth of Alabama and Birmingham Illustrated* (1886) is prefaced by one of her poems. Old-time residents of Blount Springs report that she always had ready a poem for friends whom she received on Duffee's Mountain or met on her rare visits to Blount Springs. Her correspondents frequently mention having received poems from her. Perhaps, her best known poem is "Cleopatra."[33] As early as 1888 she had attained sufficient recognition to be listed in Appleton's *Cylopaedia of American Biography*.[34] In Alabama biographical works she is listed as a poet only until her inclusion in Marie Bankhead Owen's *Story of Alabama*.[35] Here for the first time an adequate biographical summary appears.

Although Mary Gordon Duffee was better known as a literary figure outside Alabama, at Blount Springs her popularity abounded. As the years passed, she left her mountain top home only for occasional visits into the village several hundred yards away. She did not by any means, however, live an isolated existence. Protesting an article in the Birmingham *Daily Age-Herald* which labeled her a hermit, she wrote to a member of her family:

A hermit is one who dwells, solitary and alone, having no communication with humanity. . . It is a well established fact that this house has people in it nearly every day in the year. On Sunday the 8th, there were fully sixty persons here, among them the Sunday School class who came up in a body to spend the afternoon. . .

One would imagine from reading this article that my home consisted of one little room full of musty old books, and that I was utterly oblivious of the progress and passing events of the day. I doubt if there is a woman in the State who receives more papers and magazines, and keeps better posted on the events of daily life in the outside world. [This writer] also indicated that my whole life had been spent here on the mountain. I was not born or educated here, and certainly have traveled some and seen much of the U. S. from New York to New Orleans. . .[36]

Mary Gordon Duffee liked to receive these mountain-climbing visitors in the grove of trees outside her house. Her letters reveal that she held court there for the most distinguished Alabamians, who found her keen mind and store of information both interesting and valuable. She mentions in letters to her niece, Ella Duffee, the combined strain of receiving droves of people during the day and writing by the oppressive heat of the lamp at night.[37]

In addition to these daily personal contacts Mary Gordon Duffee carried on a voluminous correspondence, involving an exchange of information, pamphlets and books. For example, in one letter (1909) J. W. Worthington, president of the Sheffield National Bank, sent her the Engineer Board's report on Muscle Shoals, a pamphlet on the fixation of atmospheric nitrogen in the form of fertilizer, another pamphlet on the manufacture of calcium cyanamid in England, and a copy of two laws passed in the last legislature. By similar means she received much of the source material for her writing.

As the generation of Alabamians who had known and respected Mary Gordon Duffee passed, another generation took its place to whom the "poetess of the mountain" had become the "witch of the mountain." A photograph of her taken about 1910 substantiates this reputation. In the day of neatly swept-up pompadours, her hair falls about her shoulders. Heavy flat-soled shoes, an ill-fitting shirtwaist and skirt, and a crocheted shawl contrast her with the other women in the group. When curiosity seekers ventured onto her property, she scurried from her house to chase them off. Such eccentricities naturally added to the lore already surrounding her. She was believed to have been a Confederate spy and to have possessed documents as proof.[38] Reportedly, she brought information on foot from Kentucky to Elyton on the size of Sherman's army. Various versions of another story tell of her having appropriated a large sum of money to distribute among the needy impoverished by the Civil War.[39] It is not known whether she was guilty or assumed responsibility to shield others; however, she was arrested, but not convicted.

In her last years she was faithfully attended by a Negro couple, Maggie and Isaac Point, who brought meals through the woods from their own kitchen, as Mary Gordon Duffee would not allow a fire to be built in her house. Solicitous friends and relatives tried to move her to more comfortable quarters, but she refused to leave in spite of the dilapidated condition of her house. Finally, in 1920, at the age of seventy-six she died in a room whose roof was intact only over her bed. She was buried on Duffee's Mountain beside her mother and father. No stone marks the grave of this woman who is best remembered as the "historian of the hill country."

Virginia Pounds Brown and Jane Porter Nabers

CHAPTER 1

The carriage and wagons stood ready at the door and we embarked on our four-day journey from Tuscaloosa to Blount Springs. Annually in June my parents with my three brothers and I moved from Tuscaloosa to Blount Springs, where we operated a resort hotel.

We followed the old stage road out of Tuscaloosa, and on the rise of a hill we turned back for a last look at the University. Soon we entered a wooded district of oaks and pines onto the "old plank road," which extended sixteen miles in the direction of Elyton.[2] The first point of interest reached was a picturesque stream, Hurricane Creek, spanned by a strong wooden bridge. On the right was the embankment of the first railroad I had ever seen, then called the Northeast and Southwest Alabama, now known as the Alabama Great Southern. Tuscaloosa business men, desiring to secure the trade of this rich and fertile valley, had helped to promote the construction of this railroad. Pamphlets and speeches were made on the subject, and stock issued. These efforts, however, resulted in its reaching a halting point only a few miles from Tuscaloosa.[3]

Coal Haulers

Soon we began to meet a new and distinct phase of population in the "coal haulers," the true pioneers of the coal trade. They lived in humble homes built of pine logs, cultivated small patches of corn, peas, and yams, and dug coal wherever it was "handy to git at," never more than one wagonload at a time. They spent the whole day going to town to sell the coal for groceries and the necessary jug of liquor. To see one of these coal wagons was to see them all; generally two oxen pulled a small wagon driven by a gaunt, swarthy man, sitting upright in front, energetically bent on arriving in Tuscaloosa. On the return trip a slow plodding pair of oxen drew a wagon with no visible sign of life within. Of course, there were exceptions of thrifty men who brought home other things than the jug, but, on the average, they were a peculiar type of simple-minded humanity. The coal haulers knew nothing of geological science or research connected with the coal measure. They simply dug coal where it was most clearly exposed and estimated its value by the good it would render them in a trade with Maxwell or Glasscock.[4]

GLASCOCK & FOSTER,

Are now receiving their supply of

Fall and Fancy

DRY-GOODS,

Consisting in part, of the following :

PLAID, figured and solid colored de Laines and Cashmeres; plain black and colored Alpacas, figured alpaca : various color marino, and coberg cloth : black dress silks: colored silks and bombazines : Florence Marcellaine and glaze silks, assorted colors; ginghams: English, French, and American Prints : black and colored satins : silk monde : crape leise ; emb. muslin collars : Chemisettes and Under-sleeves : ladies white, black, and colored kid and silk Gloves : Ladies beaver gloves and gauntlets; men's beaver and kid gloves: an assortment of Bonnet, Taffeta and satin ribbons: an assortment of bleached and brown domestics and jeans: Cassimeres, sattinetts, tweeds and jeans for pants : Linseys, kerseys, flannels and blankets: ladies white, black, slate and mixed cotton hoes : ladies merino and silk hoes: men's merino half hoes: cambric, jaconet, swiss, mull and Nainsook muslin : jaconet, swiss and thread edging and inserting : an assortment of dress trimmings; worsted bands; ladies goat, calf and kid boots: ladies lasting gaiters : kid and lasting slippers, white kid gaiters and slippers : a good assortment of school shoes: walking shoes: Misses goat and kid boots : an assortment of children's shoes : rubber over shoes.

G. & F. have also on hand an assortment of Crockery and Glassware, Hardware, Cutlery and Guns, Hats and Caps, stationary and umbrellas, buckets, &c.,

☞ We will be prepared during the coming season, to buy or advance on cotton to any amount.   G & F.

Tuscaloosa, Nov. 3, 1854.   32-tf

From the Jones Valley Times, November 3, 1854

13

Iron Ore

As evening approached, we entered a pretty town with the unromantic name of Buckville.[5] The buildings had a venerable air of antiquity, and a stranger was at once seized with the idea that he stood in some old deserted village. Beyond Buckville, we passed a place known as "McMath's,"[6] with a big roomy house and fine spring. As the road crossed the hill, we had our first glimpse of the iron ore exposure at Dick Murphy's.[7] Year in and year out, he planted and gathered his crops. In Tuscaloosa he bought his plows made of English iron to use against the rocks of iron ore in his own fields. His old face showed surprise when we asked him why he didn't reduce the ores, and the next moment he smiled as he told us he couldn't, "but it was a dead sure thing to be done someday." He, like the rest, had an unfaltering faith in the development of the coal and iron industry.

Numerous primitive efforts were made by the county blacksmiths to utilize the iron ore. They constructed crude ovens and mixed lime rock with the ore, but the product was too brittle to admit heating or hammering into shape on the anvil.

The first successful attempt at iron making in this locality occurred in 1826 when a Mr. McGee of Montgomery, Alabama, built a furnace on Roupe's Creek, two miles east of the Elisha McMath place. Daniel Hillman soon purchased the furnace and operated it successfully until his death in 1831. With no railroads in the state, he had to transport the iron in wagons over rough country roads to reach the market at Tuscaloosa forty miles away. He also had the problem of unskilled and inexperienced labor in this sparsely settled district. Because of his success in mastering these obstacles, he may be justly styled the founder of the iron trade in Alabama.

After Hillman's death the furnace lay silent until 1836 when Ninean Tannehill purchased it. Tannehill was among the first pioneers who settled in the valley in 1818. His marriage to Mary Prude was the first one solemnized in the little log house at Elyton where subsequently the Jefferson County Court House stood. Tannehill operated the furnace prosperously until 1855, when he sold it to Moses Stroup.

Born in Lincoln County, N. C., in 1793, Stroup embarked on his lifelong pursuit of iron-making at the early age of eleven. He later built the first rolling mills in the South on the Broad River and made the first railroad iron used in Georgia. During his lifetime he built seven furnaces and five rolling mills. In 1852 he came to Alabama, where he built the Round Mountain Furnace in Cherokee County. Stroup ran the Roupe Creek furnace until 1865, when it was burned to the ground by Croxton's Brigade of Wilson's Raiders.[8] The wanton destruction of this furnace ruined him financially.

A mile or more from Buckville was the goal for which we had driven all day, the home of Dr. Daniel Davis, a wealthy and prominent man of the region. Behind an avenue of well-trimmed trees stood his big white house where we were welcomed for the night. We arose early the next morning to continue our journey. After breakfast and a pleasant chat, we prepared to leave, as the vehicles and teams were ready. Our host assisted my delicate mother into the carriage, bade all of us children goodbye, and grasped my father's hand firmly in his as he said, "Goodbye, Matthew. God bless you."

Cave-in

The country was more thickly populated than on our previous day's journey, and the geological features of the soil betrayed the minerals beneath. We soon came to a large field which a short time before had been the scene of a cave-in. We stopped to see it and were awed indeed by such a phenomenon, not realizing at the time that it was an occurrence peculiar to limestone formation, especially where the region is disposed to be cavernous.[9] M. C. Thomas of Tuscaloosa, whose parents owned the place at the time of the catastrophe, furnished me at a later date an accurate statement of what happened.

In 1831, William Thomas and his family were residing on their farm, fronting the main road between Elyton and Tuscaloosa two miles north of the residence of Dr. Daniel Davis. About one hundred and fifty feet from the house was a sink with a diameter of twenty-five feet. It was seemingly hard compact ground for in it were growing saplings of hickory, oak, and sassafras, and, towering above all the rest, a chestnut tree sixty or seventy feet high. One evening Mr. Thomas had the cluster of smaller growth cleared and felled the chestnut tree, intending upon the following day to cut it up into sections for rails. About ten o'clock that night a heaving, rumbling sound was distinctly heard in the direction of the sink. Next morning it was discovered that a section of the surface surrounding the sink, almost two hundred feet in diameter, had sunk to unknown depths and filled with water to within twenty feet of the top. The chestnut tree and every vestige of timber had disappeared forever. When we saw it, here and there rails and poles, protruding from the stagnant water, indicated that pressure from underneath or washings from the surface had afterwards built up the floor of the lake.

Jones Valley

We now entered a long valley called Jones Valley. The continuation of the valley to the north was known as Murphrees and to the south as Roupe's.[10] When Alabama was a territory, the entire valley was called Jones. Jones Valley and the village of Jonesboro were named for John Jones, who with his brother-in-law Caleb Friley brought the first immigrant wagon into the valley in 1816, when the whites were permitted to take possession at the termination of the Indian Wars. Those who first settled in Jones Valley along with John Jones were Andrew McLaughlin, William Prude, Williamson Hawkins, James Thompson, James Nations, Jeremiah Jones and William Roupe.

Following the old Huntsville Road, which was then an Indian trail leading from Ditto's Landing on the Tennessee River to Mudtown on the Cahaba,[11] these first pioneers located in Jones Valley ten miles south of present Birmingham. John Jones, who was generally known as Devil John because of his reckless courage, had a disagreement with a member of his party, William Roupe. The ensuing fight resulted in Jones' favor, and Roupe moved to the extreme south end of the valley, soon known as Roupe's Valley. Andrew Jones, cousin of John, arrived in 1817 in time to witness the battle between his kinsman and Roupe. Dr. Andrew Jones of Amity, Arkansas, grandson of the first Andrew Jones, writes me that his grandfather in his last years often reminisced about Jones Valley as he first saw it in its wild beauty with unbroken forest, clear streams, and the strange-looking red rocks of the mountains hanging in the crags above.

Red Mountain

We made quite an ascent by a tedious and winding road. Even the most careless observer could not fail to be attracted by the geology evidenced in the rocks on every hand. Suddenly the landscape changed, and we all halted to gaze on the mountain looming up before us—the famous Red Mountain.[12]

The Indians used the "red-dye rock" of this mountain to stain their implements and make a mixture for their favorite war paint. In the early white settlement of the valley a few remaining bands of the Creek tribe annually traversed the region from their camp at Mudtown on the Cahaba to Old Town on the Warrior on their trading expeditions in belts, cane baskets, bows and arrows. A harmless set of vagabonds, they gradually disappeared as the section became more thickly populated. The pioneers learned from the Indians to color their woolens and fabrics with the iron ore. Being easily set with a simple chemical substance, it made a lasting dye, especially for jeans, blankets, coverlids and linsey dresses.

Red Mountain extends a distance of ninety miles, is one mile wide and three hundred feet high. It is surrounded by three great coal fields: the Warrior Coal Field with an area of 5,000 square miles, the Cahaba Coal Field of 300 to 400 square miles, and the Coosa Coal Field of 300 square miles. Let me anticipate a few years and quote from a lecture delivered by Professor Henry E. Colton before the Polytechnic Association of the American Institute of the City of New York: "From Grace's Gap, Southeast, is one of the most wonderful sights ever beheld by the eye of a geologist.[13] The extreme summit of this ridge is a bluff cap of this fossiliferous ore—it looks like great massive piles of granite rock. I could not believe my eyes until I sent for a hammer, and climbing over these vast masses for miles, continually broke pieces from them. . . . There were dozens of detached pieces lying as if chiseled off, any one of which would run the largest furnace in Pennsylvania for weeks."

I quote next from an article in the Birmingham *Iron-Age,* May 21, 1884:

"In the extremities of the great Appalachian Chain . . . of Central Alabama, we found a level . . . plain extending in a northeast and southwest direction for about 30 miles in length, and from 3 to 5 miles in breadth. . . . The entire surface has a dip or inclination to the northwest which causes all its streams of water to traverse the valley in an oblique direction, and to fall into the deep trough of the Warrior River, which drains the great coal fields of the state. This inclination of the valley throws the courses of its waters against the opposing hills on its western side, and causes them to break through their rocky barriers in a series of low gaps which are guarded on either side by walls of sandstone. As the valley is watered by numerous fountains gushing from the foot of the hills, there are several large creeks that run by parallel lines along and across the valley. The principal of these are—Turkey Creek, Cunningham's, Five Mile, Village, and Valley Creek. . . .

"The soil of the Valley is the kind known throughout the Allegheny region as limestone land. It rests upon a very heavy and tenacious foundation, and grows darker toward the surface in proportion to its fertility. On this soil, in past years, large crops of cotton and the cereals were produced with little labor. It is well adapted to the grasses and especially to clover and blue grass. . . . Its vast forests on either side of the valley afford wide range for stock, and abound in deer and wild game. The streams are noted for trout . . . and varieties of fish."

CHAPTER 2

In which the Writer visits Jonesboro

~‹⊙ℍ⊙›~

We descended a hill and passed into the village of Jonesboro,[14] which was located on the banks of a creek with a view of the finest part of the valley. Not far off in various directions we could see the farms of the Jordans, Spencers, Princes, Sadlers, and other prominent families. This wealthy farm district typified the agricultural potentialities of the county, which John T. Milner describes in his book, *Alabama, As It Was, As It Is, As It Will Be.*[15] According to this book, the valley bases its claims to notoriety not only on its unequalled store of minerals but also upon its agricultural resources; just as favorable an opportunity is afforded the farmer as the miner. Milner quotes from the 1860 Census the per capita production of Jefferson County in live stock, wheat, corn, peas and beans, potatoes, honey, butter, meat, and cotton. When properly cultivated and tilled, our soil compares well in production with that of the rich states of the West.

Fruit Culture

Our soil and climate are also peculiarly adapted to the diversified culture of fruit. On the poorest hillsides crops of peaches and hardy apples are raised. The strawberry, apricot, pear, and other small fruits thrive also. The housewife dries her fruit in the sun that she may utilize its substance and flavor for her midwinter table.

In Blount County in 1817, Andrew Aldridge discovered on his place an apple tree from a volunteer seedling brought from Tennessee. He took good care of the tree, which lived to an old age and became known as the Patriarch Apple Tree. In 1828 John Fowler, who lived on the main road to Blount Springs, planted an orchard of fine East Tennessee apples. He soon began to transport surplus fruit to distant parts of the state as the fame of Fowler's apples spread. His success induced those in the hill regions of Jefferson to engage in the business, and apples became a staple county product. In 1850 not less than one hundred wagons were sent throughout the state.

In 1852 my father set out at Blount Springs on the northern slope of Duffee's Mountain an orchard of Fowler apples covering over a hundred acres. While only an amateur apple grower, as our home was in Tuscaloosa, nevertheless in five or six years he sold a large amount of apples, besides giving freely to all visitors. He cultivated only three varieties, the Pennsylvania Wine Sap, the Fowler's Winter Pearman, and the Gold Pearman (called Fowler's Yellow Pippin).

My father raised sheep in addition to apples, and the mutton on his table was unsurpassed for quality and flavor. Yet this mutton received its substance from the wild, native grasses of the rugged mountain. Even such rare foods as celery grew well in this locality. In 1857 my father won a silver cup as a premium for the largest and finest celery exhibited at the Alabama State Fair at Montgomery.[16]

Cotton

Cotton from Jonesboro went to Tuscaloosa and thence to Mobile by keelboats and flatboats. Some cotton was sent north to Gadsden and on up the Coosa River to Rome. When a line of steamboats began to operate on the Tennessee River, all cotton produced in the northern part of the state, especially in Blountsville and Brown's Valley, went to Guntersville and up the river to Chattanooga.

In 1820 efforts were made to navigate the Warrior River with small keelboats. The plan included laying out a town called Baltimore on the banks of the Mulberry Fork of the Warrior about seven miles west of Blount Springs. Many lots were sold at fancy prices, and a circular described Baltimore as the future emporium of boat building and coal mining in Alabama. A few houses were erected, and several small keelboats built, notably one by Elijah Cunningham, intended for use in trade between Tuscaloosa and Mobile. The great falls below the junction prevented the successful navigation of the river, and the town of Baltimore faded into oblivion.

Jonesboro Pioneers

On one side of the creek at Jonesboro stood an old blacksmith shop surrounded by a wagon yard for the accommodation of teamsters and countrymen who came to the village to do their trading. On the other side of the Tuscaloosa Road, which formed the main avenue of Jonesboro, lived Samuel A. Tarrant, a native of South Carolina. The leading merchant in Jonesboro, he had a flourishing trade supported by the wealth of that vicinity. He kept a first-class boarding house noted for entertainment of the traveler as well as the resident guest.[17] To this establishment were attached stables and yards for the accommodation of drivers, as Tarrant's was the dividing point on the route between Dr. Daniel Davis' and Mr. Roebuck's. For a long time Tarrant served as justice of the peace, as well as the Jefferson County representative in the State Legislature. Captain of Company H, 28th Alabama Regiment, he was forced to resign his commission due to physical limitations.[18] He then became the Confederate tax-collector for the County. The conflict left him, like so many others, financially prostrate, and at the death of his wife, Ellen, he spent his remaining days with his daughters.

Samuel Tarrant's father, James Tarrant, Sr., a native of Virginia, had commanded a company under General Washington during the Revolutionary War. After peace was declared, he moved to South Carolina, where he served as member of the committee to prepare a constitution for the state. Several years later he came to Alabama. In 1818 in Possum Valley he established at his own expense that sacred and familiar landmark,[19] Bethlehem Church, for which his slave Adam cut the logs.[20] In later years, Adam and his master often united in supplications to God.

James McAdory of Jonesboro was conceded to be the wealthiest man in Jefferson County. Even though he exacted the full measure of duty and work from his numerous slaves, he was a humane master, not regarding them merely as property but solicitous of their welfare in spiritual as well as material matters. Besides allotting gardens to each family, he provided them with comfortable quarters, an abundance of food, and nursed them when sick or aged. He always paid his slaves promptly in silver coin for their extra work. Some earned as much as a dollar a day in the cotton picking season.

Among his many slaves, Col. McAdory had a foreman by the name of Jesse, an able and smart negro, proud of his position, who never failed to exercise his authority over the "common" negroes. By daily contact with the white folks Jesse had accumulated a large stock of big words which he used liberally and indiscriminately in giving orders to the gang. On the Sabbath when attending church, he wore a full suit of the finest broad-cloth, a tall silk hat, and a ruffled shirt. This costume created awe and envy among his colored brothers and added great importance to his position, especially the next day in the fields. By thrift and good management, Jesse saved $400 in gold and silver, but when Wilson's Raiders passed through the valley, the Federal soldiers discovered his treasure and took the last cent of it.

SALEM
Male and Female Academy:
JONESBORO', ALA.

Rev. R. PHILLIPS. *Superintendent.*
HENRY F. MEEK, Principal Teacher
and Professor of Ancient Languages.

Mrs. M. A. ATKINSON. Teacher in the Female Department: A lady of long experience in teaching : a thorough scholar.
Mrs. ANNIE M. WILLIAMS, Teacher of *Music.*

THE FIRST SESSION of this Institution will commence on the 3d Monday in Sept. next, under the Superintendence of Rev. RECBEN PHILLIPS, who has been engaged in teaching and the government of Schools for 35 years; and whose skill and management of youth is surpassed but by few persons anywhere. His unemployed time in the government of the institution will be taken up in the instruction of the primary classes.

The male and female schools will be conducted in different buildings, some four hundred yards distance from each other, and the music will be conducted in a room in Mrs. Williams' dwelling, fitted up for the express purpose, and will be very comfortable. Great care will be exercised in carrying out the rules and regulations in reference to the pupils, in preserving their morals and their advancement in Literature.

It is believed by many that there is no location in the State so desirable for schools as SALEM, for good Springs, and surrounding forest, for recreation comfort and health. There is no location that affords fewer temptations to dissipation, vice and extravagance. No intoxicating liquors are kept by any person except for medical purposes. The institution is surrounded by a wealthy community, noted for their hospitality and love of morality and religious influence.

It is the interest of the Trustees to keep up a School of high order from year to year.

The scholastic year will consist of ten months only divided by a few days vacation at the close of five months from the time of commencement.

TERMS :

Tuition in Prep Departm't per month, $1 60
Higher branches, 3 00
Ancient Languages, 4 00
Music on Piano, and use of 4 50
Contingent expenses 20 cents per month.

Boarding per month for males at Col. James McAdory's (washing, fuel and lights included.) $6 00

In other families from $1 75 to 2 per week.

No student will be received for a shorter time than one session, or from time of entry until the close of session. No deduction from price of tuition will be made, except in case of protracted sickness.

From the Jones Valley Times, October 17, 1854

21

When he was freed, his fortunes went down with his master's, and he became "hard run" in his efforts to make even a scanty living, but he never lost his pride or his use of language. Years later when summoned by the sheriff to attend court, he pompously told that official "that he would not accept of the summons at all."

Thomas McAdory, brother of James, lived about two miles southeast of old Jonesboro on the Eastern Valley Road. He reared an unusually intelligent family as exemplified in the career of his son, Isaac Wellington McAdory, who during the war was a lieutenant in the 28th Alabama Regiment. He later founded Pleasant Hill Academy, which with the church became the religious and educational center of the Jonesboro neighborhood.[21] Around its familiar school grounds and altar cluster the most sacred memories of these people. There they received a liberal and polished education, and there on the Sabbath they met in devout worship.

A man of unusual talents was John Thomas, a bachelor resident of this village. He had a mill and gin and raised cocoons in his mulberry orchard. He spun and wove their silk into beautiful handkerchiefs, using the first flying shuttle in this section.

Andrew McLaughlin, a Scotsman with all the solid traits of his race marked on his face, came into the valley with John Jones and settled one mile northeast of Jonesboro. His early training on foreign soil made him utterly unprepared for the trials of pioneer life, but he had the indomitable will and pluck of his race. When he first settled his farm, he dug the trees up by the roots. Then he learned to cut them down and to make rails for constructing a fence. Proposing to have it straight and neat, he set the rails in a line, end upon end; but, after the fence reached a height of four or five rails, it fell down as fast as he made it. Weary and disgusted, he rushed into the house and told Nancy, his wife, that he was in despair because he could not make the fence stand up. He called in his neighbors, who kindly explained that a serpentine course locked the ends of the rails and enabled them to defy the strength of the wind or the power of cattle to throw them.

Once while McLaughlin was hunting on Shades Mountain, wolves attacked his dog. Never having seen such "varmints" before, he thought they were panthers, but killed four or five of them with his knife. Another time he took refuge in a tall hickory tree from a hungry pack of wolves. For five days he remained there without food or water until he was rescued. As a result of this adventure, the Indians regarded his life as charmed and called him "the white-faced wolf chief." The heather of the Caledonian hills bloomed not about his feet, but hearts as true as ever bled with Bruce or

Wallace trusted and loved him.

Duncan S. McLaughlin, the eldest son of Andrew, was one of the first four white children born in Jefferson County.[22] He is the father of Professor Felix J. McLaughlin of the Carrollsville neighborhood.

Indian Mounds

In front of the McLaughlins' were several cone-shaped Indian mounds.[23] James Adair in the *History of American Indians* tells of trading with the Indians at the old Indian Mound camping place on the banks of the creek at Jonesboro as well as at the popular trading ground at the Elyton Spring.[24] He followed the Indian camps from Rome, Georgia, to the Tuscaloosa Falls. In this book, Adair tells of millions of acres that would yield beautiful crops of corn, wheat and oats, cotton, tobacco and indigo. He describes coal lying upon the river banks where it had been washed out by heavy rains and a mountain of iron extending the length of a day's journey, hardly fifty miles from the Black Warrior Falls. William Bartram in his *Travels* relates that one of his resting places was at Mound Camp Ground at Jonesboro, where the venison was the best he had ever tasted.[25] He also camped at another favorite spot of the Indians, the beautiful McMath's Spring. The Jonesboro mounds were explored by James D. Middleton, general field agent of The Bureau of Ethnology.

Another well-known mound of the valley was on the Huntsville Road near Roebuck's.[26] Square in shape, this large mound rose thirty feet out of a level field. The walls were sloping and the sides were covered with underbrush, while massive trees crowned the summit. I regret that I never climbed to the top to discover if the mound was solid or hollow. If the former, it might have served as a council ground for neighboring chiefs or for the celebration of an important festival. If the latter, it might have been a fortification where the chief and his family were quartered while his followers camped on the adjoining plains.

There used to be an old Indian camping ground on what is called Camp Branch, a small creek running into Village Creek at the falls. It is said that the Indians came there to obtain silver from an old mine west of the camp on the head waters of Lost Creek. Old settlers agree that the Indians obtained large quantities of an ore that greatly resembled silver. Mr. Jackson Crocker, who lived on the Warrior River, said that he had often seen the trail to the mine but never the mine itself. The existence of such a mine is likely as the Indians possessed silver ornaments.

CHAPTER 3

❧❦❧

After leaving Jonesboro, our road led through a long lane and became very rocky. Close by in a dense grove of cedar and oak was located the home of David Hawkins, a member of the numerous Hawkins family who seem to have the faculty of picking out, under the guidance of their pioneer father, the fairest and most fertile spots in this valley. The approach to the front gate led over immense slabs of limestone, and on their premises flowed one of the deepest springs in the region. About half a mile northeast of this spring is a natural well, perpendicular and round as if hewn by human hands. If a wooden bucket or plank fell into this well, it soon reappeared floating on the surface of Hawkins' Spring.[27] The depth of the spring must have been very great as a stone dropped into it repeated an echo for nearly a minute.

Now began the roughest experience on all that long, weary ride of a hundred miles. For ten miles we rode over a bed of hard limestone; the only sign of soil lay in the track cut by the wheels.[28] In the center of the road protruded jagged stones, trying to the horses' feet. Many a moment I spent leaning out of the window watching the wheels roll over and over in the deep limestone rut and pitying the poor horses. The stage drivers of Powell, Jemison and Ficklin called it the Devil's Racetrack. The country teamsters referred to it as Stony Lonesome. It was the horror of all travelers and almost impassable in winter. At the end of Stony Lonesome, a sandy stretch of road led to a group of sycamore trees on the bank of a creek across which stretched a footbridge. Here we halted for our noon lunch.

Carrollsville

We entered now the old village of Carrollsyille, named for the schoolmaster, Thomas Carroll, and his brother Samuel.[29] In the early days the town was a trading center but, like Bucksville, had become a well-preserved fossil to remind the traveler of the past. Several of those peculiar and beautiful trees known as Lombardy poplars stood like sentinels, adding a foreign air to the place. In the village were several blacksmith shops with an old water mill visible in the distance. Such a place impressed the traveler with a melancholy feeling. One might tear down every house and fence, plow up the gardens and destroy the shade trees, but still an indefinable something would indicate that a community had lived here.

The Carrollsville area was settled originally in 1819 by the Joseph Hickman, William Pullin, John Brown, and William Brooks families, who emigrated from Pendleton District, S. C., and located near Brown's Spring. At that time the spring was about ten feet in diameter, deep and clear as crystal with a mantle of green moss covering the surrounding rocks and fish sporting its waters. The cabins constructed by these pioneers were little more than rail pens.

On the long weary hours of our journey my attention often rested on the variety and beauty of the flowers by the wayside. I was particularly attracted to the wild violets that bloomed in such profusion and learned that the Indians used their leaves to treat burns. They placed the leaves in a basin of warm water, and in a few minutes the whole mass became soft like a slippery elm poultice. This they laid upon the burn and bandaged it. In less than a quarter of an hour all pain had ceased, and the poultice was removed. The Indians were well versed in the medical virtues of certain plants, and their simple remedies were eminently successful.

How tenderly I love those old-fashioned flowers such as zinnias, pinks, holly-hocks, and lilacs that bloomed in the gardens of my youth. The poet, Longfellow, was so devoted to that early harbinger of spring, the lilac, that he made it a rule never to leave home while it was blooming. Only a year before his death, Longfellow was invited by a literary club of Boston to meet several distinguished Englishmen at a banquet. He replied that "he could not possibly go away while the lilacs bloomed." Beside my window at Blount Springs thrive old English lavender and bushes of sweetbrier which came from a cutting we gathered at Ruhama in the autumn of 1861. My father had known and loved the sweetbrier in his early home in Ireland and longed to have it at Blount Springs.[30] None delighted me more than the winding wisteria, climbing the rocks and empurpling the trees. I found it associated in my mind with women like Mrs. Matilda Nabers whose toil and patience made beautiful the rugged hill and sloping plain.

Mrs. Nabers, widow of Francis Drayton Nabers, had lived in her present home on the Tuscaloosa Road at Carrollsville since her marriage in 1825. Even though she had many slaves, Mrs. Nabers preferred to work her own garden. One day in 1863 while tending her flowers, she heard a rumbling of wheels and, looking toward the gate, saw a wagon drive up. Two men lifted out a strange looking box. Mrs. Nabers, going out to meet them, inquired of the contents of the box. She was informed that it contained the mortal remains of her son. She had not previously heard of his death.

Francis Drayton Nabers was the son of the pioneers, William and Sallie Nabers, whose farm was near Stony Lonesome on the ford of Valley Creek within sight of the Huntsville Road. While making his way from Madison County in North Alabama to the land office in Tuscaloosa in 1823, William (Billy) Nabers lost his bearings in the wilderness somewhere near a creek. He wandered through the woods for two weeks, and on at least ten nights his faithful horse carried him back to the same sleeping ground. Since his subsistence consisted only of acorns and twigs, he became exhausted and famished. His rescuers were afraid to give him the amount of food he craved, and in the night he surreptitiously ate the acorns hidden away in his pockets. He was finally able to resume his journey and secure land whereon he established a happy home. His friends bestowed the title of Lost Creek upon the stream of his sufferings and lonely wanderings.[31]

Pioneer Schools

The first school in Jefferson County was founded in Carrollsville by Thomas Carroll of York District, S. C., who came to Jefferson County in 1820 to seek his fortune. Persuaded to start a school in the vicinity of Jonesboro, he devoted his energy and talents to placing the enterprise on a solid foundation. John Brown furnished most of the money to build a log house at his spring in a grove of hickory trees. Among Carroll's pupils were William King, John Henley, James and John Harrison, John and William Cochran, Joseph R. Smith, and his brother William D. Smith, known in his younger days as Razor because of his quick wit and repartee. Afterwards Carroll taught school at Elyton and at Salem with Jacob H. Baker. Many young men of Jefferson County and the surrounding counties received their education from these two. The school at Carrollsville was excellent, but the life of the village was short, as Elyton had the advantage of crossroads travel and Jonesboro was located in the heart of a wealthier district.

Because the pioneers coveted education for their children, the schools of the valley generally were good. The largest school houses on the Huntsville Road previous to the Civil War were at Elyton and Jonesboro.[32] No seminars or colleges existed, but adequate schools presided over by competent teachers filled the need. The old field schools were all patterned alike: a hewed log cabin or rough plank structure housing a single large room with a fireplace for winter. Nearby was a blackberry patch, a shady grove for play, and always a switch orchard convenient for the cure of misbehavior. School was opened every morning with prayer and a Bible reading. The girls swept the floor and the boys carried water, cut wood, and made

ELYTON
Male and Female Institute,
Elyton, Ala.

Rev. JACOB BAKER, *A. M., Principal and Professor of Ancient Languages.*

Assistants in Male Department;

G. T. DEASON, *Tutor in Mathematics,*
JOHN T. CAIN, *Tutor in Anc't Languages,*
L. G. McMILLION, *Primary Department.*

Assistants in Female Department.

Rev. THOMAS F. GREEN, *Professor of Mathematics, Moral and Mental Science.*
Miss JANE A. KENNON, *Teacher in various English Branches.*
Miss VIRGINIA OWEN, *Teacher of Music.*

THE first session of this Institution commenced on the 4th Monday in January last, under the superintendance of the Rev. Jacob H. Baker, who has been for several years Principal of the Salem School, near Jonesboro', in this county, and whose em nent qualifications as a Teacher of youth are well known, and highly appreciated.

The Male and Female Schools are conducted in different buildings, remotely situated from each other, and strict regulations will be enforced in reference to the visiting of the pupils. The buildings are large and commodious. The location of this Institution will compare favorably with any other in the State.

There is no village more healthy, and none that affords fewer temptations to dissipation, ice and extravagance. By a special act of the Legislature, the sale of intoxicating liquors in any quantity, is prohibited within two miles of the town. It is the intention of the Trustees to make the Institution one of very high order, and no pains will be spared to effect that object.

The scholastic year will be divided into two sessions. The first session commenced the 4th Monday in January last and will end the last of July; the second beginning 1st of September, and ending last of December.

TERMS:

Tuition in Primary Depart't, per month, $2 00
" " Higher branches, 3 00
" " Ancient Languages. 4 00
" " Music on Piano, and use of, 4 00
Contingent expenses 25 cents per month.
Board in the best families from $1 75 to $2 00 per week.

No Student will be received for a shorter time than one session, or from time of entry until close of session; and no deduction from price of tuition will be made, except in cases of protracted sickness.

BUCKSVILLE
Male and Female High School.
Bucksville, Tuscaloosa Co.

Rev. A. C. THOMASON, A. M., Principal.
Mrs. S. C. THOMASON, Assistant Female Dep't.

THE first session of this Institution opened on the first Monday in March, under the superintendence of Rev. Mr. Thomason, who has been actively engaged in the instruction of youth, for the last thirteen years, and who was recommended to the Trustees by the Rev. Henry Talbird, D. D., President of the Howard College, at Marion, Ala.

The location is one mile and a quarter beyond McMath's on the Huntsville road, 24 from Tuscaloosa, in a neighborhood renowned for its good waters, health and moral rectitude.

The students will have frequent opportunities of attending Church within five hundred yards of the Institution, and every possible attention shall be directed to their moral, as well as mental culture.

The scholastic year will be divided into two sessions. The first session beginning the first Monday in March, and ending the last of July. The second, beginning the first Monday in August, and closing the last of December.

TERMS OF TUITION PER MONTH:

Primary Department, $1 50
English Gram'r, Arithmetic & Geography 2 00
Higher English branches,   3 00
Ancient Languages,   4 00
Music on Piano, and use of Piano,   4 00
Drawing, Painting, &c., usual rates.
Board in respectable families from $1 50 to $2 00 per week.

Students will be received at any time during the session, and charged with tuition from the time of their entrance, except in cases of protracted sickness.

From the Jones Valley Times, August 31, 1854

27

fires.[33]

Here ruled the young teacher with Webster's spelling book, a dictionary, geography, and McGuffey's reader. As there were no copy books, the teacher set all the copies. He generally was a well-educated man who had come from an older state where education was better established and teachers more plentiful. Other teachers were students struggling to earn money to complete their term in a University. As there were no public funds for education, the teachers were dependent upon contributions from the neighborhood. Having no regular boarding place, they stayed a week with each pupil until the circuit was complete. Their everyday clothing was woven and made by the women, while the men contributed to buy them a Sunday suit. During vacations, they returned to their kindred or did harvest work. If they were married, their homes were most humble.

When a community became able to build a frame or brick schoolhouse and to employ several teachers and a music teacher, an academy was established. A bell in the schooltower added to the dignity and importance of the community. The teachers who had formerly walked a mile each day now owned a horse and buggy and went driving for exercise. Moreover they had a regular place to board. Improved conditions of education were slow in coming, but evidence of continuing advancement was steady.

The wealthier classes sent their sons and daughters, after completing the course at the home school, to the institutions in Tuscaloosa.[34] Those pioneers wished to supply their descendants liberally with all the opportunities of an education which the wild condition of the country had denied them in their early days.

Williamson Hawkins

After lunch, as the road improved, we traveled faster that we might reach our overnight stop before dark. The view of the country generally was more extensive, and here and there we recognized the homes and plantations of many familiar names, notably the Brown, Hawkins and Smith families.

Over the field in an old grove was the home of Williamson Hawkins, who held a position towards the early settlers and their descendants as Abraham towards the children of Israel. He carried in his heart the fear of God but no fear of man. Coming from Tennessee about 1815, he settled near Ruhama Church but subsequently moved to a farm on Village Creek two miles northeast of Elyton. There he remained until after the War. He was a stoutly built, strong, healthy man, about average size, plain and unostentatious. His fine mind and judgment compensated for his lack of education.

When Williamson Hawkins built his cabin in 1815, he was worth scarcely a hundred dollars, but by thrift and good management he accumulated a fortune. He won from a wilderness one of the finest plantations in the state of Alabama. In those early pioneer days, he and his wife, Elizabeth Nations, overcame many hardships. Wild animals were abundant in the woods, and near his house he killed a large bear with a knife.[35] In 1816 a severe draught in the area caused even the Big Spring at Elyton to dry up, but the little band of pioneers, scattered wide apart, managed to survive and make a crop. In 1865 an invading army found Williamson and Elizabeth Hawkins living securely alone among one hundred slaves in whose devotion and obedience they trusted for safety.[36]

Slaves and Slavery

I have thought that a history of Williamson Hawkins, typical of thousands of benevolent Southern slaveholders, would have counteracted abolition stories of the fugitive slave. Planters were solicitous of their slaves' welfare to the point of mortgaging or selling land rather than breaking up a family by selling a slave. The runaway slave was exceptional, usually the laziest rascal on the place. However, being a runaway did not lessen his value, as he was frequently taken a long distance away and smuggled in a traveling traders' gang.

I express the sentiment of the South when I declare that I am glad the slave system is abolished. Negroes deserve respect for their struggle to elevate themselves, educate their children, and support their churches. I believe, however, that emancipation should have been gradual.

Among his many slaves Hawkins had several who made and repaired wagons, shod horses or mules in the home blacksmith's shop. Others made baskets to use in picking cotton; a Negro cobbler mended shoes; women spun and wove cloth. Others made tubs or pails out of the abundant cedar. Hawkins raised cotton only to provide ready cash for dry goods, groceries and necessities not produced on the farm.

The greatest trial he had to contend with, Hawkins said, was the unshaken determination of every Negro on the place to attend every circus that showed at Elyton. At one time he called them up just as they were starting to Elyton and asked if each had the necessary quarter to pay for admission. Oh, yes, they all had it. Upon his arrival at the tent, he had to expend $11.00 for forty-four tickets, as that number did not have a cent of their own.

In the old days of slavery in the valley the Negroes celebrated many holidays. Next to a meeting, a funeral or a wedding, they rejoiced in a corn-shucking and the ample supper that accompanied it. As they shucked, they boasted of their crops, told tall tales, and laughed heartily. Every corn-shucking had its leader, and Leonard Spencer was declared the vainest and finest dressed in the country. He proclaimed himself in command of the "Lower Regiment" of Jonesboro and would ride on horseback at the head of his column arrayed in a uniform, long plumes in his hat and a sword belted around him.

Runaway Slave.

COMMITTED to the Jail of Jefferson County, on the 24th inst. by T. M. Atkins, a Justice of the Peace for said county, as a runaway slave a negro man who says his name is GEORGE, and that he longs to Joseph Thompson in Williamsburg District N. C. Said boy had with him a pass dated 17th of October, 1854, to go from Green County, Alabama, to Augusta, Georgia, signed Thomas Smith. Said boy is about 28 years of age five feet six inches high, weighs about 110 pounds. The owner is requested to come forward prove property, pay charges and take him away, or he will be dealt with as the law directs.

NATHAN BYARS,
Jailor of Jefferson County
October 27, 1854. 31-tf

From the Jones Valley Times,
November 3, 1854

Hawkins' Plantation

The arrangement of Williamson Hawkins' farm was unusual. Instead of being fenced, his horse lot was enclosed on three sides by strongly built cribs, each stored in harvest time with corn and oats. The big doors always stood open; he boasted of never using a lock on his cribs. Nearby were well-filled barns and stacks of hay and fodder. He raised wheat, oats, rye, potatoes and turnips but never sold a bushel. His smoke house was filled with cured bacon; yet in the autumn at "killing-time" he had enough hogs in his pens to last two years.

When the season arrived for laying out his farm, Hawkins first of all allotted gardens and patches for each slave family; next, fields for corn, wheat, oats and rye; then fifty acres of his best land in cotton for the sole benefit of his slaves; last of all, the land left in cotton for himself. He always paid his slaves for extra work; he clothed them nearly as well as himself; and he worked harder with his hands than any of them. He chastised them as little as possible, tenderly nursed them when sick, sympathized with all their sorrows, and never severed their family ties by sale.

I honor the Hawkins' family coat-of-arms whose heraldic device is a plough. When I visit a museum, I would rather see there the plough that pioneer used the first day he broke a furrow on his little farm than the relics of military heroes.

CHAPTER 4

IN WHICH THE WRITER VISITS ELYTON

❧◉❦◉☙

As the lane became a street, we entered Elyton,[37] the Jefferson County seat of justice and the trading center for Jones Valley and the surrounding hill country. Probably because of its magnificent spring, main source of Valley Creek, Elyton had been from the first a focal point for pioneers. It became an intersection of the trailways of the wilderness and later the crossroads for north-south and east-west stage routes.

Travel from Tennessee and North Alabama flowed through Elyton en route to Tuscaloosa, the state capital and headquarters for Warrior River navigation. At Elyton eastbound traffic to Georgia by way of Montevallo, Selma, and Montgomery intersected westbound traffic to Mississippi through Jasper.[38]

Sometime in 1820, a small group of pioneer families decided to name their village Elyton, in honor of William Ely, a federal land agent. He was commissioner of the Government land grant for the Deaf and Dumb Society of Hartford, Connecticut. Mr. Ely made several trips to Alabama to select, procure, and dispose of these lands, then mostly occupied by squatters. By his business sagacity, he wisely administered his trust to the satisfaction of the inhabitants, who, desiring to honor him, chose his name for their county site.

With the exception of Jonesboro, ten miles south, Elyton was for fifty years the leading town between Decatur on the Tennessee and Tuscaloosa on the Warrior. The nearest neighbor of any importance was Montevallo, about thirty-six miles distant.

As far as bustle and progress were concerned, however, Elyton was a fitting abode for Rip Van Winkle. For many years naught disturbed its serenity: the tide of travel flowed through regular channels; planters and small farmers came in, traded, and went their way; circuit court brought its usual attendance and ripple of excitement; the big mountain of iron loomed above; still the town did not grow. Later, through its streets marched Confederate soldiers, followed by Union troops who left poverty and destruction. Then came the weary and bitter task of rebuilding. Men came with compass and chain, and soon a train roared down the valley to a new town that was being laid out within a few miles of Elyton.[39]

Dry Goods and Groceries.

AN entire new and full assortment of Dry Goods, Groceries, Hardware, Cutlery, Drugs, Boots and Shoes, being received and to arrive, to which I invite the attention of purchasers:

Dress Goods, of various styles,
Tissues, plain and striped,
Plain Swiss and Jaconet muslins and lawns,
American, French and English prints,
Brown and bleached Domestics,
Cotton sheetings, cottonades,
Brown and check Linens, pure Irish Linen,
Ladies and Gents silk and kid gloves,
Long and short net mitts and gloves,
Triming Laces: Pins and Needles,
Jackonet and Swiss Edlings and Insertings,
Lisle and Linen Edgings and Insertings,
Rich Embroided Undersleeves,
Collars and Chimezetts,
Bordered and hemstiched Hdkfs,
Ladies and misses linen, lisle and cot. hose,
White and brown mix'd 1-2 hose,
Bonnet, Neck and Taffeta Ribbons,
Black and color'd Cloth,
French Casimeres.

GROCERIES;

Brown, Clarified and Loaf Sugar,
Molasses in whole and half barrels,
Mackerel, Nos. 1, 2, 3, in whole and half bbls.
Tobacco, various qualities,
Rice, mustard and starch,
Black and green Tea,
Tallow and star Candles,
Turpentine, Linseed Oil, white Lead,
Spice, Pepper, Ginger and Nutmegs,
Raisons, Pickels and Lemon Syrup,
Cloves and Cinamon,
Indigo, Madder, Alum, Powder and Lead.

Hardware:

Trace Chaines, weeding Hose,
Plough Lines, Manilla Rope,
Axes, Hammers, broad Axes and scales,
Tea Kettles, Wagon boxes, Waffle Irons,
Rasps, mill-saw Files, Gun Files,
Cotton and Wool Cards,
Gun Caps, Violin strings,
Knives and Forks, and Pocket Knives,
Scythe Blades, Augers and Chisels,
Hand saws, shaving boxes and brushes,
Chains for Pumps and fixtures.

DRUGS.

Mustang Linement, and Pain Killer,
Radway's Ready Relief, and Paregoric,
Laudnum, and Bateman's Drops,
Sulpher, Ess. Cinamon, Ess. Lemon,
Cologne, Maccassar, Bears and Creole Oil,
Noxvemica, and Calomel,
Shaving soap, military shaving soap,
Window Glass 8 x 10 and 10 x 12,
Blacking and Putty

Hats and Caps:

Fash. Moleskin and Beaver Hats,
Boys cloth, and Fur Caps,
Panama and Leghorn Hats.

Bonnets——Silk and Straw.

Gents and boys, Ladies gaiters and walking shoes, ties and slippers and Rubber shoes.

Gents over Shoes.

Clothing:

Fine black and col'd cloth Coats,
"   "   "   " dress Do,
Marino, Alpacca, Tweeds and Drill,
Linen and Flannel Over Coats,
A great variety of Pants and Vests,
Black and col'd silk cravats,
Suspenders, stocks, coat Links,
Linen and Silk Handkerchiefs,
Umbrellas—Undershirts,
A fine assortment of Collars and Drawers

Crockery of every description.

A great variety of Books,

Pencils, Slates, &c.

I am determined not to be undersold by any other house in Alabama, with cost of transportation added. I therefore say emphatically—call and examine, before you purchase elsewhere.

JAMES A. MUDD

Elyton, April 1, 1854   iif

From the Jones Valley Times, August 23, 1854

From the Jones Valley Times, 1854

33

Corner Store

Several stores in Elyton, owned by James Mudd, William A. Walker, Sr., and Dr. Joseph R. Smith, transacted extensive wholesale and retail trade.[40] The corner store, located at the intersection of the principal roads, was the "Exchange" of Elyton. Here the men of the town and the surrounding region met to discuss finance and trade, and to exchange news in lieu of a daily paper. Under the shade of the mulberry trees, comfortable, old-fashioned split-bottom chairs were constantly occupied in good weather. A big horse rack stood in the middle of the Road for the convenience of the countrymen, and a plank walk led to the Big Spring down in the bottom.[41]

Not far from the corner store was a shabby enclosure where, disregarding the law, mountaineers from Blount County and independent citizens from the free state of Walker hitched their horses to the fence.[42] This practice made it difficult to keep presentable the grounds surrounding the courthouse.

Courthouse and Tavern

This two-story red brick building was an unpretentious structure, but it was amply large for transactions of business.[43] Its walls had echoed the splendid oratory and legal arguments of Judge Mudd and lawyers Peck, Van Hoose, Martin, Porter, Earnest, Hewitt, and Walker.

There came a time when the question arose of the removal of the county seat from Elyton to Birmingham. To many in Jefferson County the thought was profane; they shrank at the suggestion of old Elyton's surrender to the new-fledged village over in the field. "Why," said an old gourdhead dismounting from his mule that had brought him and his saddlebag from 'Possum Valley, "why, hain't they got brick and mortar enough in that 'ar upstart of a town they call Birmingham to build 'em a Court Housen of ther own without disturbin' hones' people."

Below the corner store in Elyton Joseph Hickman kept a hospitality tavern. In 1854 he had sold his farming lands to Elijah Brown and moved to Elyton where he operated a tavern and hotel for four years. He then disposed of his Elyton interests and moved to Pickens County, Alabama. Although the tavern's architectural appearance fantastically combined ornateness with pioneer simplicity, its outward visage was as worn and solemn as though it had been constructed of lumber from the wreck of Noah's Ark. The colored lady who presided over the cuisine was a famous cook. Her concoctions equalled the circulars from a Chicago Commission House. Had flour, pork, and chickens been costly, she would have bankrupted Potter Palmer, much less good old man Hickman. In addition to her other qualifications, she was the leader of society among her race, and she constantly longed to gather a bucket and hasten to the Spring to listen to the gossip at that popular rendezvous. Never did we pass the Spring without seeing a throng of servants from all parts of the village gossiping and quarreling among themselves.

Newspapers

Previous to the Civil War, a weekly newspaper, *The Central Alabamian,* was published in Elyton. Its editor, James Norment, experienced in journalism, wrote well. In his columns, he urged the establishment of furnaces and utilization of the district's mineral wealth. His faith in its possibilities, however, was not rewarded during his lifetime.

After the Civil War, Thomas McLaughlin of Jonesboro came as a young man to Elyton and established a newspaper called *The Jefferson Independent,* which he conducted with much ability. Afterwards, he moved the paper to Birmingham, where for some time it was the only paper published. In Birmingham he entered into partnership with the Irishman L. H. Matthews, who added to his duties as editor the responsible position of superintendent of education. Matthews was a forceful writer, anxious for the progress of Birmingham and the valley. The mechanical work on the paper was done by printer Ras Cantley, who loved his friends only too well and scattered his hard earnings as rapidly as he set type.

The Jefferson Independent flourished until the *Iron Age* was established. Mr. Matthews then withdrew from *The Independent* and moved to Blountsville where he edited and managed a most readable village paper. Mr. McLaughlin struggled on, soon retiring from the field.[44]

Churches

In and around Elyton church facilities were abundant.[45] The pioneers of the valley early began the erection of meeting houses for religious worship. At first, services were held in the homes of members during the winter season, and in the autumn, summer and spring at their camp grounds where tents and rude shelters gave protection. Soon plain and substantial churches without costly trappings or artistic decoration were built by the Baptists and Methodists. After the Civil War, through the efforts of Judge Mudd, Dr. Hawkins and others, a beautiful Episcopal church was built on what is now the principal thoroughfare from Elyton to Birmingham.[46] For several years the leader of the Church was Reverend Phillip Fitts, a native of Tuscaloosa. After graduating from the University of Alabama, he chose law as a profession but later abandoned it to become a minister. His wife, Sophia Holland Cochrane, the daughter of Tuscaloosa's able lawyer, William Cochrane, was one of my schoolmates.

The pioneer preachers received no salary, each church giving whatever sum it could raise. Through summer's heat and winter's cold, these men of God made their way on horseback from one church to another, stopping at farmers' houses for overnight shelter. Often they took refuge in Indians' wigwams where they were always kindly treated. Sometimes they traveled in a canoe to attend a special camp meeting. Much time was given to preaching funeral sermons, for the pioneers believed strongly in this custom. If no preacher were available at the time of death, a day was set often six months ahead when all the neighborhood from miles around should gather to hear the sermon.

Usually the preachers were men of education, sometimes, like the Reverend James Tarrant, reading Greek as easily as English. They chose their text carefully and expounded it in words that swept through the house. They wrestled fearlessly with men for the salvation of their souls and plainly pointed to them the straight and narrow path. Such a preacher was the Elder John Powers who sang his favorite hymn, *How Firm A Foundation,* until the rafters vibrated. These men went out like John into the wilderness preaching the word of life.

Elyton Pioneers

In Elyton William A. Walker, Sr., owned a large mercantile store which he operated until after the Civil War when his plantation and mills required all of his time. He was the son of Richard Walker, who resided in the neighborhood of present Coalburg. Grave and learned in appearance, William Walker was nevertheless keenly alive to everything that occurred. No man has more genuinely deserved to rise with the wave of Birmingham's prosperity, since he remained loyal to his birthplace through its reconstruction trials.

In an angle between the Montevallo and Georgia Roads was the elegant home of William S. Mudd. His father, James Mudd, had moved his family from Kentucky, and doubtless realizing the striking resemblance between the vicinity of Elyton and the Bluegrass region, located permanently here. Their home, the present residence of Dr. Joseph R. Smith, served as a popular stop for stage coach passengers, who appreciated both the hostess' delicious food and the host's genial wit. Often the stage was delayed far beyond the scheduled hour so that those waiting for friends or mail grew impatient. One day James Mudd delighted them by halting a plodding team of oxen and inquiring in a serious manner if the driver had passed the stage somewhere in the last ten miles!

This constant contact with legislators and students traveling to and from Tuscaloosa influenced the formative years of William S. Mudd's life. It was around his father's cheerful and hospitable hearthstone, listening as a child to the brightest minds of the State, that the wish to be a learned man and a good citizen first sprang up in his heart. Appreciating his abilities, his family placed him in college at Bardstown, Kentucky. Returning to Elyton, he studied law with Judge Peck and subsequently became a respected judge of the circuit court. Urged to run for governor during the political upheaval following the Civil War, he preferred a scholar's retirement. When James R. Powell founded Birmingham, Mudd, believing in the future of Jones Valley, was a cornerstone of the new community.

From Elyton, a broad street led out to Newtown.[47] Here lived Judge Wilson Sylvester Steele, a merchant, whose father was one of the founders of the coal trade in the Cahaba Field. The residence in this section that attracted the attention of the passerby because of its size and beautiful rose garden was that of Dr. Samuel S. Earle, who came to Jones Valley from South Carolina. Besides his abilities as a professional man and a planter, he was highly educated and possessed in no small degree the gift of poetry. I have never heard anyone read Burns with the intense feeling and comprehension which he threw into every verse.

To the Earle family belonged an old darkey named Ellick. He accompanied his young master, Paul H. Earle, to the Confederate Army, and served as a cook for the mess. An ardent Southerner in his sympathies, he never left his old home after obtaining his freedom and died a few years ago, having been tenderly cared for by the Earle family.

Past the spring on the left side of the road was the home of Dr. Joseph R. Smith, son of an original settler of the valley. John Smith and his wife, Sallie Riley, migrated from South Carolina to Tennessee and thence to Jones Valley in 1816. Their lands spread out on either side of Valley Creek about three miles from Jonesboro. If ever a man deserved the title of "Good Samaritan," John Smith was that man. He laid aside all of his duties and sought to aid the sick, often paying for their medical requirements and faithfully nursing them with his own hands.

Dr. Joseph R. Smith combined the pursuits of physician, merchant and planter. He devoted time and means to scientific study on reclamation of the soil of the section and to the breeding of fine blooded stock. When Birmingham was founded, Dr. Smith contributed to its progress and welfare.

From Dr. Smith's, the road ascends to a well-drained surface that no doubt will be used someday as a residential section for those who seek to escape the noise and smoke of the manufacturing metropolis. I discussed the possibility of this growth on the very spot twelve years ago with Colonel Powell and Mr. Linn. Today I am still strongly convinced of my theory.[48]

Among the citizens of this vicinity was William Earnest, well-known lawyer and farmer. He later lived on Shades Mountain where he raised fine fruits. From reading and observation he became interested in the resemblance of the geological formations of the hill country of Alabama to the vineyard areas of Italy and France. He experimented with the scuppernong until he succeeded in establishing a large and profitable vineyard from which he manufactured scuppernong wine.[49] Mr. Earnest sold the property to Dr. James Kent of Selma, who was interested primarily in the mineral resources of the valley.

CHAPTER 5

❧◉❀◎❧

After leaving Elyton, the Huntsville Road was elevated for a considerable distance, running over firm, gravelly soil through a forest of oak and hickory. This section seemed tranquil and isolated since its soil rendered it unfit for cultivation. The excellence of the road enabled us to travel at a rapid pace this pleasant route with many familiar landmarks.

Near the Huntsville Road southwest of Roebuck's was a settlement on the "Old Georgy Road" near present Avondale. Joseph Hickman built a homestead west of the present Alice Furnace out of lumber sawed by handpower with a whip saw; the floors were fastened with wooden pegs. Before he moved to Elyton in 1854, Hickman planted near the house a long row of walnut trees. One of these beautiful trees on the north side of the "Old Georgy Road" was selected years later as a possible crossing of the South and North Alabama and the Alabama Great Southern Railroad.[50]

However, long before the crossing of this railroad the Georgia Road was a popular thoroughfare to Rome, Georgia. Always in fine condition, few roads equalled it in pleasant riding. On this road east of Joseph Hickman's place lived Samuel Hall and Tyler Hardeman where low-lying hills surrounded the meadows. Later these lands became Avondale, a suburb of Birmingham, where Abner Killough and Peyton G. King had their homes near a bold spring which made Cedar Branch.

Ruhama

The neighborhood of Ruhama lay further northeast. Soon after the Creek Indian Wars were settled, Thomas Barton, Williamson Hawkins, Old Father Bayliss, and James Cunningham moved their families, horses, cows and sheep to Ruhama.[51] Here they built a substantial blockhouse for security against the few roving bands of Indians who still remained and hunted in the section. They pitched their tents and cleared the fields nearby. After the overthrow of Indian domination, these pioneers were able to locate their homes widely apart, and their blockhouse became a Baptist church and school. The school's influence under Jacob H. Baker and W. D.

Lovett was widespread.[52]

One of the earliest settlers of this section was James Vann, a typical pioneer in his industry, thrift, and hospitality. He entered as a homestead the tract of land which he later sold to the New-castle Coal Mines. One of his six sons, James Vann, Jr., was among the first to volunteer in the Confederate Army and was wounded in the battle of Shiloh in 1862. The most prominent citizen of the Ruhama neighborhood was Edmond Wood, an energetic plantation owner.[53]

SUBSCRIPTIONS PAID
(SINCE LAST WEEK,)
To the Jones Valley Times.

John P. Cowdan, Chepultepec,	$2 00
M. Duffee, Blount Springs,	2 00
Wm. Kirkland, Livingston,	2 00
Robert Worthington, Trussville,	2 00
Jas. Franklin, Conchardee, Talladega,	1 00
R. D. Cowdan, Village Springs.	1 00

From the Jones Valley Times, August 4, 1854

Oak Grove

The northeastern part of the Ruhama settlement, known as Oak Grove,[54] was founded around a Methodist Church by Judge W. L. Wilson. Although not wealthy, the kindhearted and law abiding farmers of this community prospered. A well-known pioneer of this district was William Reed, known as "Silver Billie" because he always paid cash on the spot in silver coins.[55]

Trussville

Now, my readers, come a few miles northeast with me to the fertile land on the shores of the Cahaba River. Springs rising in the mountains six or seven miles west of Springville form the two streams known as the Cahaba and Little Cahaba. Situated in a valley between the Cahaba River and the head waters of Shades Creek is Trussville, a prosperous village seventeen miles northeast of Elyton. The village acquired its name from the pioneer, Warren Truss, who came from South Carolina to the Cahaba valley when only a trail penetrated the wilderness. He reared a large and respected family, including eight sons. One of his sons, Thomas K. Truss, was the leading merchant of Trussville. During the war he commanded a company known as "Truss' Home Guards," which protected the community from the depredations of deserters and outlaws.

Before the war on the west bank of the Cahaba River, Billy Martin, Irish by descent and a native of Tennessee, farmed one of the richest plantations in the Trussville Beat, the upper part of which was an Indian farm. The old gray-haired Indian who held it when the white men took possession said he could not remember when it was first cleared, as his ancestors had planted it from year to year. The county line of Jefferson and Blount ran through this farm.

Roebuck's

Soon we descended to the basin of another arm of the valley. In front of us a bold creek flowed rapidly from a large spring known as the Roebuck Spring. Burwell Bass, who came from Anson County, N. C., in 1815, was the first white man to settle here. After the Government land sales he moved from the spring, where now on the terraced hill to the left stood the home of George James and Ann Roebuck.

Mr. Roebuck, a tall man, had the habit of throwing back his shoulders when he walked. His firmly set lips gave emphasis and decision to all he said. The particular situation of his farm compelled him to make of it a stand for the convenience and comfort of all travelers. Here the important Huntsville Road intersected a less used road to Blount Springs. In addition to transients whose day's journey terminated at this station, the drivers of numerous droves of horses and mules, cattle, sheep and hogs,[56] that annually poured down from the grain regions of Kentucky, Tennessee, and North Alabama to the cotton belt, made Roebuck's stables and barns an overnight stop. As a consequence, George Roebuck's name was known and respected from Kentucky to Louisiana.

North of Roebuck's house, the land spread out level, walled in the distance by ridges. On the right was a large white frame house belonging to James Hawkins. On the left in a grove of oak trees was the home of Richard Hudson, the efficient sheriff of the County in 1860-1862.

Backroad to Jonesboro

The road that swept around to the left between Roebuck's house and the creek led to Jonesboro. In excellent condition the year round, it was traveled especially by those who wished to avoid the mire of Stony Lonesome. Every foot of it was familiar to me as we often took the "back road" which was the same length as the main road.

A short distance from the intersection of the Huntsville Road and the back road stood the picturesque church known as Enon Camp Ground,[57] located on a ridge that terminated at the creek nearby. Here gathered crowds at monthly and quarterly meetings. I have never seen a lovelier spot. Through the vista in front was the plantation of Richard Hudson, while in the rear a wooded slope afforded pleasant rambles for lovers who went to church for other reasons than to hear Deacon Jones raise the tune or Elder Powers argue about the clime where there is no giving in marriage. I hope some day there will be a grand edifice there.

Caverns

Beyond Roebuck's we entered a rolling country with V-shaped ridges dividing the farms. Rich coal deposits lay beneath the poor soil. Here lived Thomas Friel, a thrifty Irishman. By draining the lands of wealthier planters, he had accumulated enough money to buy land in this out-of-the-way spot and to build an unpretentious home. When his fortunes seemed at their lowest ebb at the end of the war, large deposits of coal of the best quality were discovered where he had harvested scanty crops. He dug into the rich vein and was soon able with his son's help to purchase machinery to increase his profits.

Upon Friel's land was a cavern of great extent and beauty, which, if explored and measured, should be a source of pleasure and information to the people of Birmingham.[58] Someday I am going to inspect it in order to write my impressions. I should know how to comprehend and appreciate this cavern of the valley, as I spent nearly every day of the month of June, 1875, in the avenues and grottoes of Mammoth Cave, Kentucky. I well remember one sunny morning when a large party of us ventured as far as Croghan's Hall, the terminus of Mammoth Cave and nine miles from the mouth. During the day clouds arose, and a terrific flood of rain fell, causing a rise in the streams of the cave. We, of course, knew nothing of this storm while returning across Echo River, a stream usually fifty feet deep, very wide and clear as crystal, but, as we approached our landing, we failed to observe the usual light. Our faithful guides, old Matt Nicholas and William, sprang into the stream and pulled the boat with ropes while we lay down full length with the shallow boat fast filling with water. The low archway, four feet high in dry season, scraped our backs for thirty feet. We were thankful indeed when we crawled out and found ourselves in the lofty sand-covered floor of River Avenue. Ten o'clock that night when we were safe on the surface of the earth, all the clouds had passed away and the skies were luminous with stars.[59]

Clift's Mill and Rutledge Springs

The road now descended into a narrow valley between prominent ridges. Just above a ford on Black Creek was a large mill and dam over which the water fell a considerable height. This merchant mill was owned by George W. Clift, who took a genuine interest in the mineral development of the valley. His home, located across the creek, was a popular stopping place for Blount Springs' summer guests. After the Civil War had devastated the Clift home and mill, they were rebuilt by Jere Boyle, a native of Ireland, who had done some of the heaviest grading in the Cahaba Valley on the South & North Alabama Railroad. He married Helen Lee, for whom he named the village of Helena which he founded. After Wilson's Raiders destroyed his possessions there, he moved to Clift's Mill. Thereafter he built many miles of railroads in the eastern part of the state and between Selma and Montgomery. While still young, he was killed in a railroad accident.

WOOL CARDING.

PERSONS wishing their WOOL CARDED, can do so by sending the same to the Eagle Mills.   GEO. W. CLIFT.
June 15, 1854.   12tf.

From the Jones Valley Times, August 31, 1854

On a level plantation, about five miles northeast of Jonesboro and approached by the back road from Roebuck's, resided James Rutledge. His lands were located on 'Possum Creek near Bethlehem Church.[60] He was so generous and lenient to his slaves that the story is told that his old Negro foreman, George, usually gave his master at least one-fourth of the annual crop raised on the place. He managed nevertheless to raise a family of children on this moderate allowance from George.

Indian Legend

In 'Possum Valley several miles off the back road was located a village called Cape Smith's Shop, known after the war as Toadvine.[61] Two of the three Smith brothers, E. Cape and Oliver M., had filled the office of tax collector with integrity.

Until 1861, roving bands of Choctaw Indians annually visited the region near Cape Smith's Shop to obtain lead.[62] No white man ever discovered the exact locality of the mine, its extent or the method of mining. The Indian trail was marked on beech trees by images of a man pointing his gun in a firing position. As the trail reached the banks of the Warrior River, a massive beech near the water's edge showed also the figure of a man, but this one pointed his gun towards the ground in the direction of the water. During the dry season the shallow waters exposed the remains of an ancient mine or shaft, with earthen crucibles and other evidences of mining operations.

Three miles from Cape Smith's Shop the Warrior winds between hills and over rugged rocks that stem its channel. Here arose the legend of the two Indian fishermen of the shoals: when this century was as young as the moon like a hunter's bow bent for the chase, and before the blow of the pioneer's axe had broken the still hours around the wigwam door, the Indian looked down from Red Mountain on the virgin forest of the valley. Having mutually agreed to fight to the death on the banks of the Warrior, two Indian braves met armed for deadly fray. Discarding rifle and bow, they chose knives for combat. When one of the duelists dropped his knife, Silent Bear, a spectator, rushed in and prevented the continuation of the one-sided bout. The victor became so enraged that he ran to the bluff and cast himself into the river; his rival died from wounds. The Great Spirit, angry over the duel, doomed the two to sleep by day and fish as friends by night. Hence, every night, whether dark with wintry clouds or lit by a hunter's moon, wan with mist or clear beneath stars, two Indians with gigs and torches walk over the shoals to pursue their fishing. Their forms are distinct; their weapons gleam in the torchlight as they spring from rock to rock with all the lithe grace and strength of their nature and training.

Greene's

In sight of Roebuck's the Huntsville Road diverged to the left. In a valley where the meadows climbed the hills and the fields were long and level lived Robert Greene. His father, George L. Greene, had emigrated from Abbeville District, South Carolina, in 1819. He acquired property rapidly and became a stockholder in the Selma, Rome & Dalton Railroad before it reached Montevallo. Robert Greene continued to live in the roomy old family farmhouse. One of his sons, Dr. Robert Greene, served with much distinction as a surgeon in the Nineteenth Alabama Regiment. The marriage of his sons and daughters to descendants of other pioneers united several valley families: Owen, Truss, and Earle.

CHAPTER 6

⨀

Soon the aspect of the country began to change, and the fertile land lay either in narrow strips along the creeks or in basins surrounded by ridges and rocky bluffs. The first point of interest was Hagood's Crossroads,[63] a thrifty settlement with a store and church. The pioneer head of the Hagood family had cleared his fields when the wolves were still plentiful. The old homestead, like Roebuck's a beacon light to the traveler, was eagerly sought at the close of a day's journey. In these times a penniless stranger was as hospitably fed and housed as though he were a prince traveling incognito.[64]

Hagood's Crossroads was for a time the home of the Reverends John and Ira Powers, popular ministers of the Methodist Church. To comely looks and fine voices, they added fervent piety and careful study of the scriptures. They preached in that plain manner which seemed to say, "If I cannot by entreaty and prayers and tears melt your wicked souls, I ought to thrash saving grace into your sinful bodies—anything to save you from the day of wrath." Such strong appeals were seldom in vain, as converts followed them wherever they lifted up their songs in praise.

On what is familiarly called Hagood Mountain near Hagood's Crossroads was a lake covering a space of six or seven acres with an average depth of 65 feet.[65] The water was clear and full of fish. In recent years some enterprising gentlemen have added to the native stock of cat fish and perch the delicious mountain trout. The source of the lake must be invisible springs at the bottom, and the water seldom runs off from any surface outlet, except in a case of overflow from heavy rains. The surrounding locality affords fine sites for summer residences with pure invigorating air and romantic scenery. It should someday be a popular resort like the lake region of New York State. A cave of considerable size was located on the east side of the old Huntsville Road on the T. M. Massey place and another beautiful one on the creek near Thomas Fields'.

Hanby's Flatboats

In the Hagood's Crossroads section lived David Hanby, founder of the coal trade in the Warrior Field. Other pioneers in mining and shipping coal were: James W. Hewitt, whose mines were located near the mouth of Turkey Creek; Jonathan Steele and James A. Mudd, who mined near the mouth of Village Creek.

David Hanby's personal appearance suggested a fat, jolly old farmer "who lived at home and boarded at the same house."[66] He resided on Turkey Creek near the mills which he had bought from John Henry in 1822.[67] Besides his farming interests, he established and very successfully managed several coal mines. During the summer and autumn, he gave employment to a large force of men in getting out coal. During the winter, the coal was placed in huge flat boats and at the first rise in the river was floated down the Warrior. The dangers were many, especially at the Squaw Shoals above Tuscaloosa, which were so rocky and rapid as to imperil the lives of the boatmen and require the display of great nerve and skill on the part of the pilot.[68] At Mobile the coal found a ready market at remunerative price because of its well-known good quality and the popularity of Mr. Hanby.[69] He sold the lumber in the boats for firewood.

The boats were made of two immense slabs of timber carefully selected for soundness and strength, hewn to the proper dimensions, and seasoned thoroughly. These slabs were hauled to the banks, laid in parallel lines, and a strong floor of rough-hewn boards called puncheons was laid between them and securely fastened so as to resist all shocks of driftwood and projecting rocks. This floor was then caulked with melted tar to render it waterproof. A rude helm was constructed by placing a piece of grooved timber at one end; then by the aid of a long pole, the pilot steered his primitive craft, while strong men with oars were ready at the side to assist him when necessary.

Part of the boat was covered in order to protect the men, who cooked their own provisions and slept aboard. At night, if the current was deep and the moon shone, they floated on, but if there were clouds and a heavy fog, they pulled to the banks, tied up their boats, and remained in safety to daylight. Sometimes in spite of every precaution, the boat was wrecked on the treacherous shoals and the entire cargo lost, the crew barely escaping with their lives. Felix Hanby, son of David, made 112 successful trips to Mobile through the Squaw Shoals in spite of the unwieldy cargo and the absence of navigation charts. Levi Adams was the first flatboat pilot employed by David Hanby. His brother, Simpkins, made over a hundred trips through the shoals before he was twenty-eight years old; he also made three hazardous trips to Tuscaloosa in a skiff.

On this long and tedious voyage, the route as far as Tuscaloosa was wild and desolate as any streams in the west. The woods afforded wild game in abundance, and generally one of the boatmen, an

From the Jones Valley Times,
January 6, 1855

expert hunter, would take his rifle and follow the shore, keeping in sight of the fleet, until he had secured a deer or turkey.

On arriving at Mobile, the crew was promptly paid and discharged. From there they reached Tuscaloosa by the regular line of steamers, generally working their way to save their hard-won earnings. From Tuscaloosa, they took what would now be styled "the gravel train," or in a more sensible language, they walked to their homes. With their earnings, they bought such staple articles as sugar, coffee, molasses, and dry goods. With the surplus, they purchased land and hired help to clear it.

The coal was mined partly on the ridges, from which wagons hauled it to the landing place, and partly on the steep sides of the river, where it could be shoveled into the boat moored below. Labor was cheap, plentiful, and willing, and there was never any difficulty in obtaining ample help to procure and transport the coal. Provisions of all kinds were abundant, but money was scarce. Hence the money obtained by the boatmen helped the whole neighborhood, while the wonderful sights seen on the voyage afforded a theme for the returned voyager to recite for his family and friends during the long winter evenings. Simple in their thoughts and lives, they yet drew much store of happiness from such an existence.

I wish I could repeat some of their familiar songs but can only give a stanza or so:

> "Oh! Brother, stand steady and brave at the wheel,
>   Row, boatman, row;
> We're gwine down to the big Mobile,
>   Row, boatman, row.
> There we can rest if we have but a dime,
>   Row, boatman, row.
> Then we'll come home in the evening time,
>   Row, boatman, row."

And another:

> "Oh! dance, boatman, dance.
> "Oh! dance, boatman, dance,
> Dance all night til broad daylight,
> And go home with the girls in the morning."[70]

Mr. Hanby had five sons, whose names were David, Felix, John, Milton, and Jesse. They were among the first to volunteer and follow the flag of the South. Captain Felix Hanby commanded one of the finest-looking companies ever mustered into the service of the State. It formed part of the famous Nineteenth Alabama Regiment.[71] At Shiloh, it received its baptism of fire and stood, and there young

John Hanby fell mortally wounded. The gallantry of this Regiment is especially noticed in General William Preston Johnston's sketch of his father, General Albert Sidney Johnston.[72] It was mostly composed of companies from Blount, Jefferson, and Cherokee counties, and its history reads like a story from the Middle Ages. General Joseph Wheeler was its colonel, and after his promotion, its general.

In one engagement alone in Georgia, the Regiment had seven color bearers shot down, the last acting with such remarkable heroism as to receive honorable burial at the hands of the enemy. Through all its fortunes, in camp and march, and on the battlefield, the Hanbys proved true and heroic. The conquered banner never had braver or truer defenders than such soldiers as Felix and Milton Hanby, whose boyhood was passed in this upper valley.

During the War, David Hanby fed hundreds of the soldiers' families from his five mills and several farms. Peaceful in his nature and in no way personally involved in the conflict, this father of the coal trade of the Warrior met his death in a tragic manner. One day a remnant of General Wilson's Raiders, passing through the section, met a party of Confederates and fired upon them. Old Mr. Hanby, who had stopped to engage in pleasant conversation with the Confederates, was struck by a bullet and killed.[73]

Mills in the Valley

Near Grimes Spring in the Hagood's Crossroads neighborhood we passed the ruins of the home and mill of James Cunningham on the creek named for him. Born in Ireland, he immigrated to Tennessee and from that state volunteered to fight with Jackson against the Indians. Later he explored Jones Valley and settled at this wild and secluded spot amid the hills. This truehearted old soldier brought with him his religion as well as his household goods, and in his cabin home by the roar of the waterfall was preached in 1816 the first sermon ever delivered in the valley.[74] The minister on this notable occasion was the Reverend Ebenezer Hearn, whose name and labors glow brightly in the history of Methodism.

Cunningham's sons set to work building a house and clearing a field, while the father and other sons commenced the erection of a grist mill. In digging out the mill-race, they hit thick limestone that stubbornly resisted their power to cut it with hammer and chisel. Powder to blast it out could be obtained only on pack-horses over the military trail from middle Tennessee,[75] and dynamite was unknown, but the pioneers' energy was equal to the emergency. They made fires upon the top and sides of the rock until it glowed with heat; then they threw upon it quantities of water which cooled it so rapidly as to cause the rock to burst into fragments. Thus in a short time Cunningham cleared a channel. At no great distance he found mill rock of suitable strength and grit and soon had his mill ready to grind the first crop of corn ever raised in Jones Valley. For many years afterwards Cunningham's mill did the grinding for a large and prosperous settlement.

Until Cunningham and Hanby built their mills, the pioneers traveled ninety miles through forests infested by Indians and wild animals to Gunter's Landing on the Tennessee for meal, seed corn, and salt. Soon mills were constructed in various parts of the valley, chiefly on the five principal creeks.

In 1819 Jonathan Moreland built a grist mill five or six miles east of Hanby's on Turkey Creek. John Click built another mill on Valley Creek one and one-half miles from present Hillman. Revis owned a corn mill where the South & North Alabama Railroad now crosses Five Mile Creek in a gap on Sand Mountain. There a crowd of Jackson's veterans often gathered, especially on rainy days, and recalled the stormy scenes of their youth.

The earliest grist mills were adapted only to grinding corn and had no bolters for wheat flour.[76] The first wheat was raised in Blount County in 1817 by a Mr. Guthery near the head of Turkey Creek which is now in Jefferson County. Soon nearly every farmer in the valley raised, as part of his annual crop, sufficient wheat for his household with often a surplus for market.

In 1827 David Hanby built a large mill on Turkey Creek purposely for wheat with the finest millstones for grinding and first class bolters. Besides a patronage for thirty miles around, he shipped flour to Selma, Tuscaloosa, and other points. Since the local mills possessed no modern bolting apparatus, the wheat was ground into four grades of flour: a superior grade for white bread; "seconds" or "middlings" for bread, light and healthful but not so white; a third coarser grade called "shorts" for cakes, puddings, and Graham's bread; and bran for the cattle. Many thrifty housewives made starch out of the bran. There has never been but one failure of the wheat crop in Jefferson County, when a heavy killing frost fell on April 16th, 1848. Now cotton is king, and little wheat is grown.

General Jackson's Volunteers

The soldiers of Coffee's Brigade, as part of Andrew Jackson's expedition against the Creek Indians, were undoubtedly the first white men to penetrate the wilderness of present Jefferson County. When the war ended, many, like Hanby and Cunningham, returned to make their permanent homes in this beautiful and fertile land. Some of the early settlers were mere youths when Jackson's summons for troops thrilled heroic Tennessee. They faced an unknown territory with sparse population, long marches fraught with perils, and two classes of dangerous foes, trained British veterans and fearless Creek warriors.

On the eve of Jackson's first campaign against the Creek nations, the Tennessee Volunteers were encamped at Fayetteville, Tennessee. Although they knew Jackson's fame, scarcely one of those raw recruits knew him personally or even by sight. They were all in a fever of excitement to march, but especially to know if they were to go as infantry or cavalry, for they well knew that the route was long and rough. Upon Jackson's arrival, the men could not await the delay of a formal order but resolved to run a risk to obtain information as early as possible. Among their number was a shrewd, brave, and eccentric character, Joe Young, whom they managed to slip in the apartment where the council of war was being held. At the conclusion he slipped out and promptly returned to camp, rather crestfallen, with this greeting:

"Well, boys, I'll tell you we've got to go, and we've got to walk, too."

"What! Who was in thar anyway, Joe?"

"Thar was Coffee and Carroll and Colonel Dyer and an old hickory-faced fellow. I don't know who he was."

Sure enough, the poor fellows had to march on foot, and when the old hickory-faced fellow turned out to be Andrew Jackson, it was a long time before Joe Young heard the last of it. Later he cast his lot in the valley and made a good citizen.

Creek Indian War

In this section the demands for military action were limited to the few Indian settlements on the outskirts of present Jefferson County, as the Indians had not lived here but had used it for hunting and ceremonial purposes. In October, 1813, General Jackson detached General John Coffee's brigade to conquer Old Town on the east side of the junction of the Sipsey River and the Mulberry Fork of the Warrior.[77] This brigade consisted of Tennesseans noted for their skill and valor. David Crockett, later hero of the Alamo, describes the maneuver in his autobiography: "We pushed on till we got to what was called Black Warrior Town . . . This Indian town was a large one, but when we arrived we found the Indians had left it. There was a large field of corn standing out and a pretty good supply in some cribs. There was also a quantity of dried beans which were very acceptable to us and without delay, we secured them as well as the corn and then burned the town."[78]

In 1814 General Jackson sent a detachment to attack Mudtown,[79] a trading point on the banks of the Cahaba River. Many a richly laden canoe went down the Cahaba to the Alabama River and on to Mobile. As a political meeting place of the Indians, Mudtown became powerful enough to incur the wrath of the U. S. Government.

Jackson's troops encamped for the night on a steep isolated hill overlooking the town. The next morning those Indians who had not escaped during the night surrendered. Although relics of earthen pottery and flint arrowheads can be seen there, the location of the town is now simply part of a farm which has belonged successively to the Pledgers, Samuel Acton, and Isaac Johnston.

With their defeat in East Alabama, the hopes of the Creek Indians were buried. Slowly and sadly, as the mists melt from the river before the rising sun, they disappeared. An Indian legend related that when a body of large game emigrated from a territory in which it had lived for centuries, it was a sign that the human inhabitants would be driven in the same direction. The Creeks and Choctaws declared that about 300 years ago when Alabama was full of buffaloes, a terrible draught came upon the land and the rivers, so that there was no water except in small pools miles apart. The large springs continued to run only in weak streams. Thousands of trees perished, and deer, squirrels, rabbits and birds died. Buffaloes in great numbers migrated to the Mississippi River. Finally the Great Spirit sent a rain from the big waters to the south that lasted a whole moon. Yet for a long time the game and fish were so scarce that the people almost perished. The Indians concluded that the fortunes of war had given their land to another race and that they were destined to follow the buffaloes west.

David Crockett in Jones Valley

Upon the return of Coffee's Brigade to Tennessee, the men were haunted with memories of that fair valley in Alabama. Their term of service entitled them to land-warrants, and their ambition lured them to return to the land they had first seen on the line of march.[80]

In 1815, many Tennesseans came to inspect the region, some to buy land, others to locate their land grants. The United States acquired a right to the land in August, 1814, but the whites were not allowed to take general possession until 1816. Some came along the old Huntsville road, which was originally an Indian trail leading from Ditto's Landing on the Tennessee River to Mudtown on the Cahaba. David Crockett was among those who came looking for land. He tells in his autobiography his experience in Jones Valley: "We passed through a large rich valley, where several families had settled, continued our course till we came near where Tuscaloosa now stands. Here we camped as there were no inhabitants, and hobbled out our horses for the night. About two hours before day we heard bells of our horses going back the way we had come. They had started to leave us. At daylight I started in pursuit of them on foot and carrying my rifle which was a very heavy one. I went ahead all day, wading through creeks and swamps, and climbing mountains but could not overtake the horses. I gave up the pursuit at last, and from the best calculations I could make, had walked over fifty miles. Next day I returned on my track till near midday, when I became sick and could go no further and laid down in the wilderness. Soon Indians came along. They signed to me that I would die in the forest —a thing I was confoundedly afraid of myself. I asked how far to any house. They made me understand it was a mile and one half. I got up to go but when I rose I reeled like a cow with blind staggers, or a fellow who had taken too many horns. One Indian proposed to carry my gun. I gave him a half a dollar and accepted his offer. We got to the house by which time I was pretty far gone. I was kindly received and put to bed. I knew but little that was going on for about two weeks, when I began to mend from the treatment of the good woman. She was the wife of Jerry Jones, and she thought I would die anyhow if she didn't do something so she gave me a whole bottle of Bateman's Drops,[81] and it threw me into a sweat and I immediately got well."

This Jeremiah Jones, a cousin of Devil John Jones, had brought his family into the valley in 1815 and made a crop near the present Woodward furnace.

After his recovery Colonel Crockett and his party journeyed through Stony Lonesome. From Elyton they went along the Huntsville Road as far as Mt. Pinson and crossed the river at Cook's Ferry. Soon they arrived at the sulphur springs to rest a few days as the guests of Luther Morgan,[82] whose establishment consisted of a wigwam covered with bark near two large birch trees, to one of which a large pet bear was chained. Crockett returned to Tennessee via Bearmeat Cabin and Huntsville.

Soldiers under Jackson who later came to Jones Valley were William Perkins, Thomas and John Barton, Jonathan Simmons, Draper Revis, Thomas James, Benjamin Tarrant, John Hanby, Robert Baird, and James Cunningham. They made good soldiers on the field of war and good citizens in time of peace.

Land Sales

When the lands had been surveyed and mapped, the immigrants were able to locate the sections wherein their claims lay.[83] All the lands were sectioned in 1817 and 1818. Not until July 19, 1819, did the United States Government hold a land sale in Huntsville.[84] The Government sold each tract for as much as could be obtained, usually

$5 to $10 an acre with $2 as the minimum. One fourth the purchase price was paid down and the balance in three equal annual installments, bearing interest from the day of sale. Farming lands only were wanted. Mineral lands were looked upon with scorn and were carefully avoided by homeseekers.

Among the emigrating Indians, there were a few astute men who realized the mineral value of the land they were forced to leave. Generally in the presentation of their claims to the United States Government at Washington, the Indians estimated the value of their land for hunting and fishing or agriculture. However, Major George Lowery of the Cherokee delegation surprised his audience by a recital of the immense deposits of coal within the Indian domain in Tennessee, Georgia, and Alabama, predicting that the day would come when these minerals would prove to be most valuable. He told the officials at Washington that if he had the money he would open coal and ore mines and build a furnace.

In the Huntsville land sale tracts were of equal size, 160 acres, and no limit was put upon the number of tracts one person could buy. In this way large bodies of land were accumulated by a few men who had ready cash. At that time there was no law permitting the settler to obtain his tract by residence and cultivation. If he hadn't money to make the first payment, he lost it.

On the land sale day the pioneers, to their astonishment and dismay, were met by a gang of speculators who had gotten the numbers of the most valuable tracts and those already occupied. This group boldly told the pioneers that they intended to bid a certain price which in each case was much higher than that anticipated by the settler, who must either lose his home or compromise with the sharks by paying to them the difference between their price and that of the Government. On several large plantations in Jones and Roupe Valley, compromises cost as much as $500 or $1000; in the mountain region from $50 to $100. Although too late to protect many who had suffered from graft, the Alabama Legislature in the autumn of 1819 passed acts against this system of fraud.

In those days it was difficult to make enough money to pay off land debts. Men split rails for 40c a .day; the best class of farm laborer received $8 a month. Corn was 30c to 40c a bushel; smoked bacon 5c a pound; butter 8c; honey 6c. There was no sale for eggs, and chickens sold for 10c each. Under such circumstances the prospect of the loss of farms because of inability to meet payments was so wide spread that the Alabama Legislature petitioned Congress for relief laws prolonging the time of payment. The most substantial assistance, however, resulted from an act in 1821 which permitted the land owner to relinquish a part of the tract of land in payment for the portion retained.[85]

CHAPTER 7

⟨⊙⟩

Not far beyond Turkey Creek lay the village of Kennelsville, which consisted of only two houses, one on each side of the dirt road. In one lived a rich widow, and in the other, the Jack Gills.. Their son, James Gill, or Jim,[86] as he was familiarly called, became the most expert and famous stage driver in the state of Alabama. A magnificent looking man of six feet two, he weighed two hundred and sixty pounds and towered like Saul over any crowd. Curly hair and a long jet-black beard further embellished his grand appearance. Mounted in the box with the reins in his strong hands, he was a sight I shall never forget.

Previous to the War, Jim Gill moved to Shreveport, Louisiana, and engaged in the livery stable business. From there he drifted to Texas and became wealthy driving a stage over the prairies. At last he fell into ill health. One day when the train stopped at Warrior Station, a broken old man got off. He had been dazed by the sight of Birmingham, for it looked more like the West with its rush and roar than reposeful old Jefferson County. He did not even know that the train had passed along the same road over which he had driven so often like a god in his chariot. The new generation did not recognize the old man, but finally kindly Uncle Billy Jones, taking the traveler by the hand, said, "If I am not mistaken, you are Jim Gill."

When Jim Gill drove the stage in Alabama, not a railroad operated regularly in the state. Steamboats plied the navigable rivers, and stage coaches followed regular schedules between the principal towns. The main line ran from Tuscaloosa through Elyton to Huntsville, with a branch route serving the summer vacationists to Blount Springs. Jemison, Powell and Ficklin and Company employed a small army of men to operate these lines efficiently.[87]

The heavy coach, usually painted black and gold or deep red and gold, was mounted on bright red wheels. The driver, protected by a dashboard, sat on a high box under which valuable parcels were stored. A foot brake at his side could be pressed to lock instantly both hind wheels. In the rear a covered platform, called the "boot," held the passengers' baggage and the mail. An iron rail extended around the top of the coach for the protection of small parcels or such ad-

An 1860 handbill from collection of Robert Jemison, Jr.

venturous passengers as chose to perch there.

In the coach, seats in the front, middle, and back accommodated nine passengers. Doors on either side afforded easy entrance to the passengers, who mounted on steps which folded into the doors. Leather curtains, lined with fine cloth, could be let down over the windows in wet weather, or rolled up on fair days.

The coaches were constructed in Troy, New York, and Concord, New Hampshire. To say that his stage was "a first class Troy build" was the proudest boast of the driver. Four strong horses, sometimes six, depending on the weight of the load, were needed to pull the coach. Since the body was mounted on springs, the coach produced a rolling motion similar to that experienced at sea, often producing nausea in the inexperienced traveler.[88] Every ten miles along the route, the Company established stations, consisting of a tavern and stables. Here teams were relayed and trappings thoroughly inspected. The coaches ran at night as well as in the day on a well-devised schedule.[89]

Among the equipment was a polished bugle on which the driver played a single air upon arrival and departure. When the first sound of the bugle was heard in the distance, the men of the village congregated around the tavern and post office to welcome the passengers and receive their mail. The stage driver flourished his long lash, the eager steeds trotted their fastest as the coach rolled up. Tossing his reins to the waiting boy, the driver dismounted and unlocked the "boot" to deliver its contents to the postmaster. He mounted his box when all was ready and gazed down at the humble hostler with much haughtiness.

Much depended upon the nerve and skill of the stagecoach driver. He was always well paid and hospitably entertained along the route. The agents respected him; his passengers courted his favor. Back home he was the oracle of the neighborhood, bringing the latest news of the day. He loved his calling and was proud of it.

Hill Farmers

From Clift's mill the road led north through a wild and broken country thinly settled with small farms in narrow divides between sharply defined ridges. Neat, substantial log cabins manifested industry and comfort, but not wealth, for the soil of the rugged surface through which our route lay was not fertile like that along the old Huntsville Road.[90] We were now on what Milner so aptly styled "the selvage of the valley." As the limestone began to disappear, the rock and timber implied a different geological formation from that which we had traversed for many miles. In time rich veins of coal would be discovered here.

57

With the change in the appearance of the land came an equally great change in the character and habits of the people. They loved their land, toiled for it in forest and field, and fought for it in battle. They measured no man by his wealth but by his conduct. The prototype of these people in the Tennessee mountains has found a champion in Charles Egbert Craddock.

Uncle Billy Grimes' Crooked Creek home was typical of the thrifty and independent hill farmers. The massive double log house with porches and shed rooms was surrounded by commodious stables, cribs, garden, and orchards. With the help of his children and neighbors he had cut down and hewed out of the forest trees the logs for his house, and had found material for his chimneys in the abundant rocks nearby. Logrolling and house-raising such as this provided as much occasion for social gathering and neighborly cooperation as corn shucking or less laborious undertakings.

After a ride of several miles a clearing appeared, and the road became a lane, bordered on either side with a thicket of persimmon trees. Although equal to the date in sweetness if properly harvested and cured, persimmons are neglected like many treasures of bountiful nature in the South. The fruit is usually left on the tree until frost transposes its taste from alum into sugar. Delightful to human beings, it furnished a favorite repast to the coon and 'possum abroad at night. Persimmon timber is hard and compact like ebony and when well worked by mechanical skill, presents a beautiful appearance. The tree grows rapidly and luxuriantly on poor soil, yields heavy crops, and requires little attention. I believe that one acre cultivated in persimmon trees would provide more profit than an acre of corn at eight or ten cents.

The Jacks' Place

On this persimmon-bordered lane lived James Jacks.[91] In 1836 this place, then owned by John Harris, was a stage stand and toll gate. Mr. Harris erected the mills on Five Mile Creek which he sold in 1850 to George W. Clift.

Across the lane from James Jacks' house stood stables surrounded by orchards and cotton fields, while further north was a blacksmith's shop. Beyond the forest was what old man Jacks called "my lower plantation." The homestead consisted of two large rooms built of hewn logs, well chinked and daubed, with a huge chimney in the middle. In front a wide porch ran the full length of the house; in the rear a dining room and kitchen joined onto shed rooms. Behind the house were the cabins of slaves and vegetable gardens.

In the middle of the front porch stood a large loom built of heavy timber, a web of cloth hanging on its beam. A saddle and a side saddle hung on stout pegs driven into one of the logs.

The company room was allotted to us. In addition to chairs and tables, and three large bedsteads, several barrels stood in one corner. Shelves piled with coverlids and blankets reached almost to the ceiling. New homespun dresses hung on a row of pegs. Scattered about were bunches of herbs and sassafras roots. Under the beds bags bulged with wool and cotton while over the joist balanced several pairs of old breeches stuffed with cotton for spinning in the long winter. A piece of white domestic with verses and an American eagle crudely embroidered in turkey-red thread covered the table.

Hung on the wall were woodcuts and cards printed in huge letters, R.R.R., which means Radway's Ready Relief, the famous king cure-all of those days. A flashy-looking almanac related the amazing virtues of the proprietor's special remedy, Vermifuge. In spite of the confusion of appointments, the traveler felt an air of solid comfort.

James Jacks, the head of the family, was a robust man with a florid complexion. Invariably he wore chestnut-colored jeans, the snowiest of homespun shirts, and home-knit woolen suspenders. A silent man and an inveterate tobacco chewer, he sat in a huge armchair on the porch with his eyes fastened on some distant object. The Jacks' three "yeller dogs" were held in awe by the neighbors and travelers, whose first exclamation was, "Howdy, Mr. Jacks, please keep the dogs off us." After rousing himself from his reveries, he arose, gathered a huge stick, and silently escorted his guests from gate to house. His only conversation consisted of a query about the weather.

To me the treasure of the whole place was Daddy, Mrs. Jacks' father. In his youth, he had fought in the Revolutionary Army; in the prime of life he had settled here in Alabama amongst the "Injuns and bars and wolves and sich like o' varmints." He was the oldest man I ever knew. Infirm, he sat in the corner of his little room on a chair covered with a soft tanned sheepskin. The disjointed sentences of his wandering mind betrayed much that was entertaining in connection with his pioneer days.

Sallow-complexioned Mrs. Jacks, low and thick in stature, contrasted strikingly with her husband. Her regular features wore an expression of discontent and regret quite discouraging to the stranger. She generally wore a cotton suit spun and woven by her own hands. She showed us to our familiar room with the remark "to wait on ourselves if we needed anything."

When we were seated on the benches around the supper table, Mrs. Jacks poured out the coffee, sweetened each cup with her own standard of measurement, then remarked in a stern, deep-set tone:

"Help yourselves. There's a dish of cold bacon and beans; some folks likes 'em and some folks don't; you can eat 'em or let 'em alone, just as you please. We always has 'em for dinner and I saves 'em for

Great Southern Remedy,

JACOB'S CORDIAL!

For all Bowel Diseases, Cholera, Dysentery, Diarrhœa, Cholera Morbus, Bilious Cholic, Cholera Infantum.

Also admirably adapted to many diseases of Females: most especially painful menstruation The virtues of JACOB'S CORDIAL are too well known to require encomiums:

1 *It cures the worst cases of Diarrhœa.*
2 *It cures the worst forms of Dysentery.*
3 *It cures California or Mexican, do.*
4 *It relieves the severest Cholic.*
5 *It cures Cholera Morbus.*
6 *It cures Cholera Infantum.*
7 *It cures painful Menstruation.*
8 *It relieves pain in the back and loins.*
9 *It counteracts nerveness and despondency.*
10 *It restores irregularities.*
11 *It dispels gloomy and hysterical feelings.*
12 *It's an admirable Tonic.*

☞FOR SALE, in EYTON, by
JAS A. MUDD
Aug 4. 1854   19y.

DR. MA TIN ROBERTS,
Botanic Physician,

Residence near Blackburn's Store,

Jefferson county, Alabama.

Where he may always be found when not professionally engaged.
June 10. 1854.   11tf.

From the Jones Valley Times, August 4, 1854

supper because I hate to see anything wasted. I think it's a sin to waste victuals in the sight of the Lord."

"You are quite right, Mrs. Jacks," said my father with a politic mingling of Irish blarney and genuine courtesy. "We are always happy to stop with you because you feed so well, and we hope to find your health restored."

"No, it ain't by a long jump. The last bottle of Radway's Ready Relief I took never done me a bit of good, and my liver and stomach is just as bad out of order as ever. I think I'll make the old man carry me down to Elyton to see Dr. Smith. He keeps up with all the new fangled medicines of the day, and by going down I can save paying him the mileage for riding all the way up here."

Although "crobid" from ill-health and unpolished from lack of opportunity, Mrs. Jacks possessed many admirable traits: frugality, industry, and charity. She was unusually kind to me and singularly liberal. Once I stopped with a group of friends to purchase some peaches and pears. After measuring the fruit and receiving payment for it, she gave me all I could take, including nectarines which she had refused to give or sell to the others.

Again in later years I passed this way under sad and trying circumstances. She treated my companions with haughty scorn, made me go in the house and partake of a nice lunch, followed me to the gate, and wept over me at parting.* She saw nothing wrong in my having bestowed food and raiment on starving families of soldiers, even though I risked my own life and defiantly awaited my fate.

I shall never forget the place, its inmates, and especially the big "yeller dogs." Nor the quaint truehearted old lady who stood at the gate in that last earthly interview and cried to the Friend of the hungry and suffering to shield and comfort and save me.

Indian Trail

An ancient Indian trail made an approximately level road from Jacks' old homestead all the way to the river hills. As a general thing, an Indian trail varied little from a straight line and often took an east-west course. I have noticed how clearly defined nature keeps the evidence of an old wagon road or bridle path long years after it has been fenced up or abandoned. Even weeds seem to avoid growing where the soil has been pressed by passing feet. Still plainly visible, this nearly straight Indian trail ran from Talladega across the Cahaba Valley to the Cahaba River at McComb's Ford. It then crossed Shades Valley near the head of Shades Creek and Jones Valley from the head of Village Creek on the east to Boyle's Gap on the west. It terminated at Arkadelphia after crossing the Warrior River at Nail's Ford. Long after the settlement of the country by white men, large groups of Indians traveled it in single file, as it doubtless had been their route for centuries.

From the Weekly Independent, Birmingham, November 17, 1877

CHAPTER 8

❦❦❦

To the commercial world of the 1850's Alabama was known
as one of the great cotton-producing states of the South. As
in other slaveholding areas, agriculture was the chief pursuit.[92] Manufactures were few, and little attention had been
paid to the important question of developing the state's physical resources.

Mobile, a leading cotton port, was the metropolis of the
state. Every bale of cotton raised south of Sand Mountain
went to Mobile's warehouses. The farmer of Jones Valley
necessarily regarded Mobile as the final point of destination.
Since it was his only market, he must accept whatever rates
its merchants laid down. This monopoly affected the interests
of the greater part of the producing classes, since, because
their cotton went to Mobile, all their foreign staple and fancy
groceries came from there. After the Selma, Rome & Dalton
Railroad reached Montevallo,[93] a large quantity of cotton
went by rail from Montevallo to Selma and thence by steamboat to Mobile. Before the construction of that railroad,
however, all the cotton raised in Jones Valley was hauled on
wagons to Tuscaloosa, then put on steamers to Mobile. So
important was this wagon trade to the town of Tuscaloosa
that a railroad to connect it with Elyton was discussed for
many years.

Northeast and Southwest Alabama Railroad

Early in the '50's[94] the survey and construction of the
Northeast and Southwest Alabama Railroad was begun.[95] It
proposed to penetrate the cotton belt to the Mississippi line,
tap Tuscaloosa, the head of navigation on the Warrior, pass
through the mineral regions and terminate at Chattanooga.
Stock and money were liberally subscribed along the whole

route. I remember the enthusiasm in my native town Tusca-loosa when the chief engineer of the railroad arrived with his staff. As a little child led by my father's hand, I witnessed for the first time the ceremony of breaking dirt to commence the railroad. The whole town turned out for a holiday.

The railroad progressed slowly, however, and did not reach Elyton until after the lapse of many eventful years. The name was changed to the Alabama and Chattanooga Railroad after Stanton had assumed management of its construction, and now it is known as the Alabama Great Southern.[96] When the last rail was laid and the last spike was driven, the state was in a measure bankrupt. The tremendous resources of iron and coal in Jones Valley were still known to the outside world only through a few scientists and tourists. A neat depot building at Elyton alone stood forth.[97]

South and North Alabama Railroad

Since the entire energies and capital of the population were bent upon the purchase and cultivation of the fertile lands under the prevailing system of slavery, manufactures before the war consisted of only a few cotton factories and other minor industries totally out of comparison with the capacities of the state and the needs of the people.[98] Some sawmills dotted the pine regions, producing a supply of lumber which found a ready market among the farmers, who paid for it in cotton. Grist mills supplied the local wants of their neighborhoods, but the finer grades of flour were imported from the North and West. The sorghum molasses industry was confined largely to the poorer classes among the hills and on the pine lands. A few cabinet shops struggled for existence making and repairing furniture; the wagon and carriage business was small. One or two plow factories thrived briefly. Stroup, Hillman and others dug iron ore and reduced it at remote and isolated localities under trying obstacles.[99]

The people of Alabama were convinced, however, by the reports of geologists and mining experts that their state held marvelous resources of coal and iron. To reach these deposits, uncover and utilize them were the first steps toward profitable industry. For at least ten or fifteen years preceding the war, public and private debate revolved around the mines of iron and coal and the importance of their prompt development.

A railroad, first known as the Alabama Central and later as the South and North Alabama, was conceived with a view towards establishing industry in the mineral district. In all the newspaper articles, pamphlets and speeches made in its favor that one fact was plainly set before the people. The hearts and brains which cradled this plan were ambitious for the reclamation of the idle mineral lands otherwise worthless, but they were also loyal to the general welfare of the whole state. The railroad, chartered in 1854, would unite the resources of the cotton region of the Alabama River, the vast pineries, the mineral regions, the fruit section and the fertile basin of the Tennessee River.

John T. Milner

John T. Milner was appointed to demonstrate the feasibility of a route over the rugged hills from Decatur to Montgomery.[100] An able young engineer, he started from Montgomery to seek a path through the wilderness, crossing the heart of the mineral region, on to Sand Mountain and down to the banks of the Tennessee. In 1858 Milner toiled faithfully, and his report on the subject created new interest in the hills of iron and coal that would border the line of the road.[101] Widely copied in the press of this and other states,

Milner's report influenced to no small extent the destinies of Jones Valley. Enthusiasm grew through the entire region over the prospect of connecting the two chief agricultural regions of the state and opening up the domain of hitherto inaccessible minerals. Every energy was bent towards the success of the project.

Before the war an old-fashioned barbecue was held to draw people together to hear brilliant speeches in favor of building the South and North Alabama Railroad and developing the mineral region. The time was midsummer at Blount Springs, which place was then under the proprietorship of Matthew Duffee.[102] It was a favorable time to gather representative men from all sections and solicit their subscriptions as well as to arouse the people to a full sense of the importance of the road to all classes. Invitations were issued and preparations made on a liberal scale. The success of that day bore a strong and lasting influence on the destinies of the road.

The spot chosen for the barbecue was one of wild beauty known as the Cold Spring, which rose out of the sands close by the margin of a bold creek. A terraced hill made a sweep like the curve of an elbow, and from its base massive stones were parted in an arch, forming a cavern of grottoes with glittering stalactites and stalagmites. The lofty room of this cave was used for over forty years as a storehouse for the beef, mutton and butter of the hotel table.

Near the entrance to this cave by the large cold spring was the upper end of a long line of tables. The speaker's stand was in a little valley, making of the whole an amphitheater. The day was warm and cloudless. A vast throng gathered there: the yeomanry of the mountains in wagons, on horseback and afoot; the guests of the hotel and the summer cottages in their magnificent equipages. Men from every town in the state met there, listened, and then liberally subscribed to the building of the road.

After Milner's report was accepted,[103] books of subscription opened and stock taken, a construction force was placed in the field. The heavy grades among the hills of the Cahaba between Elyton and Calera engaged the employment of their chief contractors, Boyle and Kennedy, in order to reach Elyton from the southern terminus and begin the erection of iron works on a large scale.[104] The drums that beat the Confederate call to arms seemed, however, to echo the death note of this popular enterprise. While so much valuable work was suspended, the sound of pick and shovel might still be heard in the neighborhood of Brock's Gap where the indefatigable Boyle maintained his headquarters.

Although projectors of the South and North Railroad had dreamed of furnaces and foundries turning out material for the useful implements of peace, they little suspected that the first establishments would be built by a military power for the production of ordnance guns and stores to defend their homes. Had this line been completed and in running order at the beginning of the conflict, Jones Valley would have been an important strategic point as a basis of supplies and avenue of transit.

Oxmoor

When the blockade of all Southern-ports to commerce and the wall of armies to the north emphasized the need of the Confederate government for materials for the munitions of war, the people of Alabama realized the importance of Jones Valley. Iron was needed not only for military purposes but also for the demands of farm and workshop. The question of building one or more furnaces in the vicinity of Red Mountain became one of regional significance. The unfinished condition of the South and North Railroad made the construction of a furnace there a herculean undertaking. No individual or corporation would have dared such an effort without government aid.[105] In spite of the obstacles in transporting materials and machinery, works were built at Oxmoor. Other similar operations were Brierfield, ten miles west of Jemison Station, the Shelby Furnace, eight miles east of Calera and a rolling mill at Helena.[106] Whatever effect the safety and permanence of these furnaces might have had on the destinies of the Confederacy was prevented by the successful raid of Wilson's army which swept out of existence every vestige of these works that could be destroyed by fire.

I want to paint a picture of Oxmoor as I saw it in the month of April, 1865. The surrounding country then partook of the characteristics of a wilderness and was sparsely settled. Agriculture was the sole occupation of the people of the valley, since the minerals had up to that time been deemed worthless. The beauty of the location was striking. The sides of the hills were covered with a luxuriant growth of native forest; the waters of the creek wound around the mountain base. A path climbed the sloping ascent between the cottages of several families.

Confidence in the ability of the army of Tennessee to keep the foe in front stimulated steady work. The reverses of Hood in Tennessee and the triumphant march of Sherman to the sea caused universal gloom over the South and made more remote sections uneasy for their own safety. A raid through Alabama and middle Georgia was not suspected, however, in spite of the iron works of Jones Valley and the Confederate supply sources at Selma and Montgomery. With intent to destroy these supplies and to surround an already disabled weary remnant of the Confederate Army, General Wilson marked Oxmoor as an objective point.

In early spring a vast cavalcade of artillery and well-mounted cavalry marched across the state from Mississippi, leaving a trail of want in Walker County. They entered Elyton, scattered death and destruction over the houses of the valley and laid Oxmoor in ruins. A small force was sent to Tuscaloosa where the University was burned; the main column marched to Montevallo where General Forrest gave them a skirmish, thence to Selma.

During March I had passed through Oxmoor, peaceful and hospitable. On the afternoon of April 13 I gazed upon a scene of ruin upon this same spot that makes me shudder now as I recall it. I was in Montevallo when the invading army entered. All of my brothers were at the front, my parents at Blount Springs sixty-five miles away. About sunset rolling drums and prancing horses in a long column approached Montevallo. All night we waited, knowing a battle was imminent, as the forces of Forrest, Buford and Roddy were on the southern outskirts. Firing began at the depot, and a heavy skirmish ensued. Two days afterward **Miss Emmie Bailey** and I organized a band of women and children to go down the railroad to Brierfield to search for the wounded and dying.

Then I resolved to make my way home by foot. I met starvation on every hand and was grateful for the hominy and buttermilk graciously shared with me. After a walk of thirty miles I reached Oxmoor at the close of a tenderly beautiful day of early spring. There I hoped to receive food and shelter to relieve my hunger and fatigue. As I neared the familiar scene, my heart sank at the strange stillness of the landscape. Here and there a broken-down army horse searched for tender young grass. Wild blue flags and wild honeysuckle bloomed among the rocks. The tranquillity was overwhelmingly lonely.

At last I mustered courage to venture on and found myself standing by blackened ruins, against the wall of the furnace tower. As I contemplated the silent houses up the hill, the deserted road, the awful truth flashed upon me in despair. In alarm for my personal safety, blinded with tears, I knelt and prayed.

Rising, I saw smoke issuing from a chimney at the summit of a high hill. Wearily I climbed the steep and rugged path to this sign of security. I did not presume to ask for food, only a sleeping place on the floor. The kind head of the family was a son-in-law of old man Moses Stroup, the pioneer iron-maker. He and his family welcomed me graciously and shared with me what little they had.

Refreshed by a night of unbroken sleep, I rose at an early hour. I soon found myself at the door of Bayliss E. Grace. The following morning we parted and through a lane of mud and water I made my way to Elyton. But ere I retired that night I knelt and dedicated my future life to the glory of my native state.

The South and North Railroad After the War

Let us look at the line of the South and North Railroad in 1866. The picture is a desolate one. After the termination of hostilities gaunt poverty strode through fenceless fields;

meal ran low in the barrel, and barns were empty; veterans who had faced the guns of battle were conquered by the poverty in their own homes. The men who had projected the railroad were bankrupt in fortune, still more so in hope, and broken in heart. Briers grew over the gradings; bridges were decaying and falling to pieces. The once lively camp of Engineer Boyle could be located only by the charred remains of horseshoes and iron ties of an old cart wheel. The graded track swept around the sides of the hill at Grace's Gap. Where once stood the massive furnace, only rock walls and blackened, fire-twisted remains of machinery existed.

For many years the fate of the road had seemed doomed to death and decay. Thus affairs remained until the demands of commerce re-emphasized the necessity of penetrating the mineral region. The contractor who attempted to rescue the road was Sam Tate,[107] an experienced railroad man formerly with the Memphis and Charleston Railroad. In April, 1869, he assumed the contract to build the entire line, but the state was unable to meet its obligations. Overpowered by circumstances, he finally relinquished his contract to the Louisville and Nashville Railroad.[108]

Albert Fink, vice-president and general manager of the L. & N., believed that the South must meet the demand for diversified industries. He revealed the possibilities of the railroad as a freight carrier when the mineral regions should be developed. He made a tour over the entire line, listened to Milner, and upon returning to Louisville, recommended to the L. & N. the immediate construction of the road. He admitted that the venture was purely experimental to be solved only by tireless industry. He gathered innumerable statistics on the iron and coal deposits, forecast the founding of a great industrial center in Jones Valley, and planned a home for his thrifty race of Germans upon Sand Mountain.[109]

CHAPTER 9

With the assured completion of the South and North
Railroad came the hour for the founding of the industrial
city so long dreamed of. There could not have been gathered
in a state a circle of more financially prudent men than
those who formed the Elyton Land Company. How often
have I wished that a painting such as Leonardo da Vinci's
"Last Supper" might have been done of that long table in
B. P. Worthington's upstairs room around which gathered
the founders of Birmingham. In this room with maps on the
walls and glass cabinets of minerals, the artist might have
fixed the eagle gaze and snowy hair of James R. Powell, the
judicial repose of William S. Mudd, the striking features of
Josiah Morris, the dark hair and mustache of Henry M. Cald-
well, the handsomest as well as the youngest-looking of the
assemblage, and his secretary, Willis J. Milner.[110] In bitter
years of apparent failure these men never faltered as they
looked across to Red Mountain from which furnaces to come
might be lighted.

James R. Powell

I have now assumed the task of relating the remarkable
career of James R. Powell. My acquaintance with him as my
father's friend began when I could scarcely lisp his name.
During my school years his letters cheered me and urged me
to win honors. Through the war which saddened and dark-
ened my life he never faltered in his friendship. When the
severe climate of New York forced my return south in 1874,
he summoned me to Birmingham and appointed me the
official historian of his life.[111]

Let me describe Colonel Powell as he appeared in those
days when he was called the "Duke of Birmingham." He was
above medium height, careless in dress yet elegant in manner.

James R. Powell

His complexion was rosy, and he never wore a beard. His snowy white hair flowed long about his neck. In repose his expression was stern with a set mouth, but no one could smile more quickly or more charmingly. He was a man who would attract attention in any crowd. There was something imperial about his presence; he bore himself like an Indian chieftain.

Colonel Powell always carried a cane. On the streets when his fierce temper overcame him, he did not hesitate to use it. He was undoubtedly born to command, but unfortunately he was too conscious of the fact and brooked no rivalry. Liberal in acts of charity, he nevertheless knew the value of money. Though an aristocrat by birth, his sympathies were with the laboring class.

Colonel Powell's genius lay in his knowledge of human nature. He could read a man at a glance, size him up, and know just where to place him. A favorite saying of his was the "right man in the right place." Another characteristic was his strategic planning. He undertook a business venture involving several thousand men as carefully as a general planning a campaign. Born without fear, he hesitated at no possible danger, nor did he think of the risk involved for others. To a certain extent he was vain, for, if he originated a scheme and carried it to a successful execution, he wanted credit for doing so. He believed strongly in the power of printer's ink. He frequently remarked to me that the progress and the prosperity of the state lay in the hands of the editors more than any other class. He looked and planned far ahead of his day. The word "future" occupied a prominent place in his conversations and official documents. Had there been less temper and more patience, less ambition and more resignation, he might today be walking the streets of his beloved Birmingham.

James Robert Powell was born in affluent circumstances in Brunswick County, Virginia, in 1814. Here he resided until age sixteen when his father, who had given security for the debts of a neighbor, was compelled by his conscience and by law to yield every dollar of his fortune and render his family penniless. James Powell, though preparing for a college course, lost no time in vain regrets. He moved his parents to a small farm, and with the assistance of one negro man he worked in the fields and garden, and in the evenings he taught his sisters.

Like many another unsuccessful at home he dreamed of a distant land. At that time Alabama was the shrine to which Virginia emigrants turned. Young Powell could not afford stage coach fare, but by extra work and economy he accumulated enough money to purchase a horse and a genteel suit of clothes and still had fifty dollars for traveling expenses. Thus equipped, he started forth in the autumn of 1833 on his long and lonely journey to seek an old family friend, Henry H. Worthington, in Lowndesboro, Alabama. Before reaching Montgomery, Powell had lost all of his money but five dollars by indiscreet horse trading. In Lowndesboro he found to his dismay that Mr. Worthington, principal of Lowndesboro Academy, was leaving for Meridian, Mississippi, to edit a paper. Powell had hoped to complete his education under him besides earning a few dollars to remit to his family in Virginia. He returned to Montgomery and found a friend in Abner McGehee who listened to his story and loaned him a thousand dollars. With this money Powell leased the Planter's Hotel and sent for his family in Virginia. The hotel reopened under the style of Addison Powell and Son and soon became a popular hostelry. When his father became ill, the family moved to Lowndesboro. After one year there, young Powell took charge of the McIntosh Hotel in We-tumpka and took his family with him.

Soon the active mind of James Powell sought new fields, and in 1837 he went to Washington to bid for mail contracts in the southwestern section. Upon arrival in Washington he discovered that the stage coach had been robbed which contained his guarantees, required of each bidder by the Post Office Department. As expedition was required, he sought interviews with his former congressman from Virginia as well as his representative from Alabama. He won their confidence, and they went on his bond. He was awarded the contract for a tri-weekly hack service between Montgomery and Talladega. On July 1, 1838, he put the first hack on this important route.

James Powell achieved marked success as owner and operator of this line notwithstanding determined opposition from well-established firms. In one instance, a rival business built a fence across his road and stationed armed men to defend it. Powell equipped himself and his friends with axes and proceeded to disperse the guards and demolish the barriers. The success of his operation was due also to his attention to every detail of the comfort and convenience of his passengers. He used only the choicest hacks and horses, the most skilful drivers and the best regulated stands. He not only had a large public patronage but succeeded in raising the character of the stage business in Alabama.[112]

Within a few years Powell expanded the lines from Montgomery via Gadsden to Guntersville and Huntsville, and from Kingston, Georgia, via Rome to Decatur, Alabama, including the steamboat line from Guntersville to Decatur. He concentrated his North Alabama staging at Gadsden, where he operated daily four-horse post coaches to Rome, Georgia, Guntersville, Montgomery and Elyton.

In addition to his business interests in the South Colonel Powell took a prominent part in the establishment of the "Overland Mail Route" to California. He considered investing all his capital in that project and making San Francisco his permanent residence. The gathering storm of war, however, influenced him to defer his plans.

With the outbreak of war, Colonel Powell, having achieved success and pecuniary reward, desired to dispose of his staging interests. The Postmaster General of the Confederate Government solicited him to re-establish mail communication with Texas. Others had bid on this service but on terms so high that the Government could not consider it. Colonel Powell, in spite of his previous determination, agreed, because of his patriotism to the South, to operate the line for one-half the money named by the other bidders and to get it running within one-half the time.

In six months time the line was thoroughly established and equipped, safely carrying the thousands of pounds of mail which had accumulated between the suspension of U. S. mails and Powell's revival of communication. The entire Southwest, especially Galveston, Houston, and San Antonio, depended on the success of his undertaking for their business and military correspondence.

With this enterprise on a solid foundation Powell sold it to responsible parties and turned to disposing of his staging interests. He invested the proceeds in real estate and transportation in Montgomery. His lines had covered five states; he owned five thousand heads of horses and employed over one thousand men. His employees feared him, but they also loved him, although he required absolute obedience to his orders.

During the War, Colonel Powell evidenced his patriotism on every hand. He mounted a cavalry company at his expense and added five hundred dollars for further necessities. His elegant mansion was always open to Confederate soldiers and was the headquarters for the Confederate generals when Montgomery was the capital. Since he was a personal friend of Jefferson Davis, his social attentions to the president of the Confederacy were numerous and on a princely scale. Colonel Powell's counsel on matters of state was as much sought as though he were a member of the cabinet.

He supplied the hospitals of the South with ice when

northern sources of supply were blockaded. An unusual freeze during the winter of 1863-64 caused ice a half-inch thick to form on the Alabama River. Powell worked day and night for three days with a large force of men and drays to cut the ice and store it. Even though he was offered one thousand dollars for the ice, he refused to sell it and the following spring presented all of it to the Confederate Government for use in the hospitals.

In 1866 Colonel Powell, wishing to protect his wife and six-year old daughter from the evils of Reconstruction, closed his home in Montgomery and went to Europe with his family for an indefinite stay. He had always wanted his daughter to have an European education, and his ample means afforded opportunity for this indulgence. The family settled in Italy, occupying a winter home in Rome and a summer villa on the bay of Naples.

The restless spirit of Colonel Powell could not brook idleness, however, and he longed to return to his native land to help restore its wasted fortunes. During his tour of Great Britain he had made a special study of the iron districts of England and Wales and of the industrial cities of Sheffield and Birmingham. He met prominent manufacturers and iron makers there and awakened in them an interest in the wonderful mineral regions of Alabama. His visit to the shipbuilding city of Glasgow, Scotland, inspired in him the dream of a similar industrial port on the Gulf of Mexico. Here the iron and timber of the South could be utilized to create a commercial and naval marine.

The more he dwelt upon his observations the more determined Colonel Powell became to return to Alabama and to put his talents and money into the creation of a manufacturing city at some point in Jones Valley. Upon its success would follow the shipbuilding mart. For the people of the South to regain any degree of prosperity Colonel Powell knew that they must abandon their old methods and cease to depend solely on agriculture, especially cotton. They must diversify their pursuits by reducing the size of their farms, cultivating a variety of crops and establishing mines and manufacturing for the employment of the rising generation.

Colonel Powell believed firmly in the abilities of the coal measures to supply the commercial and domestic uses of the states adjoining Alabama. Far in the distant future he beheld a canal, either in Nicaragua or across Panama, through whose waterways the same coal might seek the shores of the Pacific. He knew that the South could never hope to make more than a toilsome and humble living amid its ruined homes and fenceless fields. It must go to the coal and ore mines, dig, delve and manufacture, and emulate the skill of its northern brethren.

In England and Wales Colonel Powell had seen coal hoisted from the collieries and loaded in vessels for a journey around Cape Horn to the Pacific. He had seen iron mined in the Cleveland district shipped around the Cape of Good Hope to the marts of India and Asia and to his own Alabama. Wandering as a tourist in the wine districts of France and Germany, he recalled the numberless hills and valleys of his own home adaptable to similar production.

Such visions as these haunted his brains and thrilled his heart as he strode along the Appian Way in Rome and contemplated the faded glories of the Caesars. Unable to restrain his impulses longer, he bade adieu to his family, embarked for America, and hastened to Montgomery. There he set about the grave experience of reducing his theories to practice by founding in Jones Valley an industrial metropolis in whose final success he never once doubted, in whose service he never faltered, and whose triumph is a lasting monument to his name.

Sale of Lots at Birmingham

The survey of lots in Birmingham, Jefferson county, Ala., at the intersection of the Alabama & Chattanooga, the South & North, the Memphis & Savannah and the Mobile Grand Trunk Railroads, being well advanced, I will, on and after June 1st, sell lots in Birmingham on moderate parties who will improve them at
J. R. POWELL,
May 20   President Elyton Land Co.

From the Elyton Sun, June 10, 1871

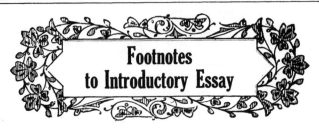

Footnotes
to Introductory Essay

1 This paper was read at the annual meeting of the Alabama Historical Association, Mobile, April 25, 1953.

2 John Milner, *Report to the Governor of Alabama on the Alabama Central Railroad* (Montgomery, 1859).

3 Ethel Armes, *The Story of Coal and Iron in Alabama* (Birmingham, 1910), p. 119.

4 Sir Charles Lyell, *A Second Visit to the United States of North America* (London, 1849), II, 79-81.

5 Marie L. Brown, *A Social History of Tuscaloosa from 1816 to 1850* (unpublished Master's thesis, University, Alabama, 1930), pp. 25-26. During these years of prosperity Matthew Duffee went to New York to pay off debts incurred in the less prosperous 1830's. His creditors, appreciative of Duffee's integrity, presented him with a silver pitcher, properly inscribed with their gratitude (Julian Duffee to the authors, Mobile, Alabama, April 21, 1952).

6 James F. Sulzby, Jr., "Blount Springs: Alabama's Foremost Watering Place of Yesteryear," *Alabama Review*, II, 166-167 (July, 1949).

7 See, for example, July 14, 1854.

8 *U. S. Census* (Seventh), 1850 [Original MSS Returns], Alabama, XII, 324, shows Matthew Duffee, 46, born in Ireland; Martha, his wife, 38, born in Tennessee; and four children born in Alabama, William, 17, George, 15, James, 12, and Mary, 6.

9 Mary Gordon Duffee, "Sketches of Alabama, Jones Valley" (typescript from Birmingham *Iron Age*, 1885-1886, 1909-1910, Birmingham, 1937, in Southern Collection, Birmingham Public Library). Hereinafter this work will be referred to as *Sketches*.

10 Minnie T. Lane to Mary Gordon Duffee, Birmingham, Alabama, May 21, 1911 (in Duffee papers, private collection of Walter G. Duffee, Birmingham, Alabama.) Unless otherwise indicated, all MSS cited are in this collection.

11 Montgomery, Alabama, November 16, 1908. Unfortunately, neither Mary Gordon Duffee nor the Department had a complete file of the *Sketches* at that time, and the missing numbers were not located until years later. In 1937 the *Sketches* were typed from the newspaper files and placed in the Department of Archives and History. Later another copy was made for the Southern Collection, Birmingham Public Library.

12 See Armes, *op. cit., passim;* Rhoda C. Ellison, *Early Alabama Publications* (University, Alabama, 1947); and Minnie Clare Boyd, *Alabama in the Fifties* (New York, 1931). Early histories of Jefferson County rely heavily on the *Sketches.*

13 *Ibid.*, II, 79.

14 *Ibid.*, II, 57-58.

15 Joel C. DuBose gives an account of the first navigation of these shoals by flatboat in Armes, *op. cit..*, p. 54.

16 Michael Tuomey, *Second Biennial Report on the Geology of Alabama* (Montgomery, 1858), p. 95 n.: "Mr. Hanby's account of his attempts at the introduction of Alabama coal into the Mobile market, would furnish an amusing chapter on the difficulty of directing any trade from its accustomed channels. The intelligent proprietors of the gas works in that city, however, were not slow to recognize its value as a material for the manufacture of gas. Much of what has heretofore been carried to market, under the name of coal, included everything that resembled it in color; but I know from observation, that those engaged in the business at present

take every reasonable precaution to reject all impurities."

17 *Sketches*, I, 89-93; II, 20-21. This sketch continues with a description of the simple lives of the crew and includes the following folk songs of the river boatmen:
>"Oh! Brother, stand steady and brave at the wheel,
> Row, boatman, row;
>We're gwine down to the big Mobile,
> Row, boatman, row.
>There we can rest if we have but a dime,
> Row, boatman, row.
>Then we'll come home in the evening time,
> Row boatman, row."

>"Oh! dance, boatman, dance.
>Oh! dance, boatman, dance,
>Dance all night til broad daylight,
>And go home with the girls in the morning."

Phillip H. Gosse, *Letters from Alabama, U.S.A.* (London, 1859), pp. 305-306, gives other boatmen songs.

18 *Sketches*, I, 10.

19 *Ibid.*, II, 154-155.

20 *Ibid.*, II, 146-152.

21 *Ibid.*, III, 451.

22 *Ibid.*, III, 474-480.

23 *Ibid.*, III, 498.

24 John L. Kerr, *The Story of a Southern Carrier: The Louisville & Nashville* (New York, 1933), p. 37.

25 *Appleton's Cyclopaedia of American Biography* (New York, 1888-1901), II, 247.

26 Birmingham *Age*, December 11, 1887.

27 See, for example, April 5, 1873.

28 Mary Gordon Duffee to John Milner, Blount Springs, June 7, 1873: "My impressions of Birmingham and its surroundings will be given through the columns of the New York *Weekly* and *Semi-Weekly Tribune* (Greeley's paper) to which I will hereafter be the Alabama contributor." Harry W. Baehr, Jr. *(The New York Tribune Since the Civil War*, New York, 1936, pp. 31-36) states that the *Tribune* received local news from "all quarters of the globe" from local correspondents, infinite in variety, whose material was either initialed or pseudonymous, rarely signed in full. The Duffee letters contain copies of Mary Gordon Duffee's correspondence with the Leslie publication in 1882. In this same collection are letters to her concerning her articles in *Youth Companion* and subscription information.

29 Mary Gordon Duffee to Ella Duffee, Blount Springs, Alabama, January 8, 1917: "Years ago I wrote up the L. and N. R. R. from Louisville to New Orleans."

30 Interview with Mary Gordon Duffee's nephew Walter G. Duffee, Birmingham, Alabama, February 15, 1953. *Appleton's Cyclopedia, loc. cit.*, states that Mary Gordon Duffee wrote a "Guide to the Mammoth Cave, Kentucky" and guide-books to various interesting places along the Southern railways. A *Bibliography of Mammoth Cave* (1924) by Willard R. Jillson, geologist of the State of Kentucky, lists an anonymous pamphlet, *L. & N. R. R. Subterranean Wonders*, a copy of which the authors have seen in the New York Public Library and believe that Duffee wrote.

31 *Sketches*, I, 104-105.

32 Mary Gordon Duffee to Ella Duffee, Blount Springs, October 11, 1910.

33 *Library of Southern Literature* (Atlanta, 1909), XV, 129.

34 II, 247.

35 (New York, 1949). III, 208-210.

36 Mary Gordon Duffee to Mrs. E. G. Duffee, Blount Springs, May 15, 1904.

37 Mary Gordon Duffee to Ella Duffee, Blount Springs, October 14, 1908.

38 Birmingham *Ledger*, July 5, 1913.

39 Interview with W. W. Moore, Blount Springs, February 4, 1953.

Footnotes to the Sketches

2 The Jemison family of Tuscaloosa built this road to their saw mill above Hurricane Creek to facilitate the haul to market (*Autobiography of James Robert Maxwell*, New York, 1926, pp. 29-30). From 1848 to 1854 the Alabama legislature chartered thirty-five companies, which built approximately 150 miles of plank roads. However, it was soon realized that the ease of construction was not sufficient asset to offset the expense of building and upkeep. The mounting interest in railroads just before the Civil War increased the dissatisfaction. See Thomas M. Owen, *History of Alabama and Dictionary of Alabama Biography* (Chicago, 1921), II, 1130-1131, and Peter A. Brannon, "Post Roads and Stage Coach Travel," *Alabama Highways*, I, 5 (May, 1927).

3 The conception and development of the Northeast & Southwest Railroad are dramatically presented in the columns of the *Jones Valley Times* (Elyton), 1854. At a barbecue at Elyton on July 12 Dr. L. C. Garland, the president of the road, delivered an address, subsequently printed in full in the issues of July 29, August 4 and 12. At this and other barbecues at Jonesboro, Ruhama Church, Hagood's Store and Trussville, $68,000 was subscribed. Often pledging slave labor instead of money, the planters in the valley seeded "immense quantities of wheat for the purpose of giving them time to put most of their force on the railroad." Ground was broken on December 7 in Tuscaloosa County, but the construction work proceeded slowly and was ended by the Civil War. In 1877 the railroad was bought by an English syndicate and became known as the Alabama Great Southern Railway.

4 *The Southern Business Directory and General Commercial Advertiser* . . . (Charleston, 1854), I, 25, lists as general merchants in Tuscaloosa: Glasscock and Foster; Maxwell, T. J. and R.

5 Michael Tuomey, *First Biennial Report of Geological Survey* (Tuskaloosa, 1850), p. 15, also spelled the word Bucksville. The town was probably named for the Buck family, some of whom are buried on a hill across the present highway from, and north of, the Bucksville Cemetery. Buck's Store is listed as a postoffice in 1827, and Bucksville, in 1830.

6 This was the home of Elisha McMath. It is noted as a location of brown iron ore in Tuomey, *op. cit.*, p. 15, and Hodgson's *Alabama Manual and Statistical Register for 1869* (Montgomery, 1869), p. 104. McMath's is listed as a postoffice in 1842 and Elisha McMath as postmaster.

7 "At Murphy's, the ore crosses the road in a bed 25 or 30 feet in thickness; and that it is not a superficial deposit may be learned by a slight examination of a ravine near the spring" (Tuomey, *op. cit.*, p. 15).

8 "In March, 1865, General H. H. Wilson set out . . . upon a raid to Central Alabama, the object of which was to destroy Confederate stores, factories, mines and iron works. Wilson moved his army in three divisions along different routes. They all met near Elyton, March 29, and destroyed iron works there" (Albert B. Moore, *History of Alabama and Her People*, New York, 1927, I, 534).

9 Duffee is correct in her geological explanation. "Sinks" and "cave-ins" are common in Jones Valley.

10 This north end was named for Daniel Murphree, who came to the valley from

South Carolina in 1815 (George Powell, *A Description and History of Blount County*, Tuscaloosa, 1855, p. 21).

11 The main Indian trails were often difficult to distinguish from hunting paths. Many, however, were widened into roads during the white settlement. The chief trails in this locality were the north-south one described here and the east-west trail from Georgia, which extended through Coosa Old Town, Cahaba Old Town, and crossed the Warrior at Squaw Shoals. See Moore, *op. cit.*, I, 351-353.

12 Toumey, *op. cit.*, p. 9, affirms the name of Red Mountain in technical terms as "a name . . . derived from the bed of red oxide of iron, that is nearly always present."

13 Grace's Gap was named for Bayliss Earle Grace, who in the 1840's dug from his farm a two-horse wagon load of iron ore which he took to the furnace of Newton Smith in Bibb County, the first Jefferson County ore to be smelted and hammered into bars. This is the present site of Spaulding Mine of Republic Steel and Iron Company.

14 Jonesboro, named for John Jones, grew up around a crude fort erected by the first settlers as protection against the Indians. It was the first colony in Jones Valley.

15 (Montgomery, 1876), pp. 24-27.

16 *Jones Valley Times*, April 22, 1854, states, "Our old friend Duffee . . . dropped in upon us last Thursday morning, looking the personification of a Boniface. Our friend was on his way to Blount Springs, to look after his vegetables, (of which he is so fond of cultivating.)" Three months later, on July 22, the paper added, "Mr. Duffee left at our office last Wednesday a very large beet, . . . a tremendous beet, weighing 6½ pounds."

17 *Ibid.*, July 1, 1854, states, "Persons loitering up this valley . . . will find a most agreeable and comfortable stopping place . . . at Jonesboro. The Hotel there and its accommodations are very good. . . . The qualities of the good land-lady are perceptible all over the house, and particularly in the good anti-dyspeptic biscuit, you will get at S. A. Tarrant's Hotel in Jonesboro."

18 The 28th Alabama Regiment was organized March 29, 1862. It was exceedingly active in Mississippi, Kentucky, Tennessee, and Georgia and finally surrendered at Greensboro, N. C. Three companies of this regiment came from Jefferson County. Their captains were: William M. Nabers; William Miller, resigned; John C. Morrow, resigned; G. W. Hewitt, wounded at Murfreesboro and Chickamauga; J. F. Tarrant, resigned; W. M. Hawkins, killed at Murfreesboro; William R. McAdory, killed at Mission Ridge; William A. McLeod, killed at Atlanta. See Willis Brewer, *Alabama: Her History, Resources, War Record, and Public Men.* . . . (Montgomery, 1872), pp. 634-635.

19 Possum Valley was officially changed to Birmingham Valley at meeting of business and civic leaders in Oneonta (see Birmingham *News*, October 20, 1946).

20 Anson West gives a similar account of the founding of the church by Reverend Tarrant in *History of Methodism in Alabama* (Nashville, 1893), p. 292. He states that Tarrant came in 1819 and built the church in 1820.

21 In 1866-1867 Professor McAdory combined the Bucksville and Salem Academy student bodies with his own in the log school house at Pleasant Hill (M. V. Brown and J. P. Nabers, "Origin of Certain Place Names in Jefferson County, Alabama," *Alabama Review*, V, 185, July, 1952).

22 Florence H. W. Moss, *Building Birmingham and Jefferson County* (Birmingham, 1947), p. 87, lists the first five children born in the section: Moses Field, December 24, 1816; William Carrol Eubank, February 3, 1818; Joseph Riley Smith, February 6, 1818; Duncan Stuart McLaughlin, March 1, 1818; Martha Prude Sadler, March 31, 1818.

23 Cyrus Thomas, "Report on Mound Explorations of the Bureau of Ethnology," in *Twelfth Annual Report of the Bureau of Ethnology, 1890-'91* (Washington, 1894), pp. 290-292, describes these mounds as the Tally mounds and gives plat of same. The Alabama State Museum and Geological Survey of Alabama explored them in 1935. A list of Jefferson County mounds and prehistoric works is given

in *Handbook of the Alabama Anthropological Society, 1910* (Montgomery, 1910) p. 46.

24 (London, 1775), *passim*.

25 *Travels Through North and South Carolina, Georgia, East and West Florida* . . . (London, 1794), *passim*.

26 William Gesner, "Mounds, Workshops, and Stone-Heaps in Jefferson County, Alabama," in *Annual Report . . . of the Smithsonian Institution . . . 1881* (Washington, 1883), pp. 616-617, lists three mounds which were on the north side of Village Creek and visible from the Huntsville Road. Gesner's location by township and range of the mounds is that of the Roebuck Golf Course.

27 Hawkins Spring, also called the Big Blue Spring, was a well known early landmark of the county. Horse and mule drivers used it for watering, and for many years it supplied water to Bessemer. It is located on the super-highway between Birmingham and Bessemer (Moss, *op. cit.*, pp. 35-36).

28 Tuomey, *op. cit.*, p. 17, makes a similar comment: " . . . the limestone . . . makes its appearance along the road at intervals between Bucksville and a point a few miles north of Elyton . . . as the strata are rather thin and worn by the wheels of vehicles passing over them, they appear like a series of curbstones rising above the surface." These outcroppings of limestone may be seen from the old Bessemer Road between the super-highway and Powderly.

29 Mrs. Kate Eubank Blackburn stated that Robert Eubank named the community Carrollton in honor of General Carroll, under whom he had fought in the "Mexican War." Eubank's son, born in 1818, was named William Carroll. Since the Mexican War was not until 1846, the writers believe that the general to whom Mrs. Blackburn refers must have been Major-General William Carroll, who was Andrew Jackson's Inspector-General (see M. V. Brown and J. P. Nabers, *op. cit.*, V, 182-183, July, 1952).

30 "Our friend Duffie on his way from Blount Springs to Tuscaloosa, on Wednesday last, presented us with a most magnificent bouquet, fresh from his Mountain Garden at the Springs. It was a rare collection of sweet flowers—roses, of every hue and tint; pinks of most delicious perfume—such a rare and odorous combination of flowers we have rarely seen" *(Jones Valley Times,* April 29, 1854).

31 W. I. and Lucy Brown tell a similar version of the naming of Lost Creek by their father, William Brown, who was lost there (in "Brown Family History," in "Historical Collection of Jefferson County, Alabama," typescript, 1937, in Southern Collection, Birmingham, Alabama, Public Library).

32 In spite of the fact that in 1818 Congress provided that a sixteenth section in every township should be set apart for school use, Alabama public schools were not organized into a system until 1854. In 1840 out of 1,053 pupils in the county, only 350 were in public school. Privately financed schools compensated for the lack of public schools. Philip Henry Gosse, *Letters from Alabama, U.S.A.* (London, 1859), p. 43, wrote: "Some half-dozen planters of influence meet and agree to have their children educated together, each stipulating the number of pupils to be sent, and the proportion of the expense to be borne by himself. These form a board of trustees, who employ a master at a fixed salary, and though they allow others to send their children at a certain date, are yet personally responsible for the whole amount . . . of their stipulated subscription." The Jefferson Academy in Elyton was incorporated in 1822, and in 1830-1831 it was divided and chartered as two schools, male and female (see Stephen B. Weeks, *History of Public School Education in Alabama,* Washington, 1915, pp. 18-19). The *Jones Valley Times,* 1854, *passim,* carries advertisements of the Elyton Male and Female Institute and the Salem School at Jonesboro.

33 Gosse, *op. cit.*, pp. 43-44: "My schoolroom is a funny little place, built wholly of round, unhewn logs, notched at the ends to receive each other, and the interstices filled with clay; there is not a window, but, as the clay has become dry, it has dropped or been punched out of many of these crevices, so that there is not

want of light or air. . . . The desks are merely boards, *split*, not sawn, out of pine logs, unhewn and unplaned, which slope from the walls, and are supported by brackets. The forms are split logs with four diverging legs from the round side, the other side being made tolerably straight with the axe."

34 In 1860, in addition to the University of Alabama, there were in Tuscaloosa three female institutes: Tuscaloosa Female College, Alabama Central Female College, and Alabama Female Institute (formerly Mrs. Stafford's Seminary).

35 *Jones Valley Times,* April 1, 1854, relates that in 1816 Williamson Hawkins encountered an enormous bear (where Elyton is now). He had left his rifle at home so decided to drive Bruin to the nearest cabin two miles away and secure a gun. He found a gun but no powder, so he took an axe and attacked the bear, "and at a few blows the monster lay dead at the feet of the intrepid woodsman."

36 Jefferson County was one of the smallest slave-holding counties, only 31% of family heads holding slaves in 1830. By 1860 this had dropped to 19%. In the Elyton Beat, where Williamson Hawkins lived, there was an average of 12 slaves per holder. Hawkins' real estate was valued in 1850 at $15,000, which made him one of the two wealthiest men in the county. See W. S. Rutledge, "An Economic and Social History of Ante-Bellum Jefferson County" (unpublished M.A. thesis, University of Alabama, 1939), p. 55.

37 Formerly known as Old Town or Frog Level, Elyton was incorporated December 20, 1820, and named for William Ely, who came there to sell lands which Congress had granted to the Connecticut Deaf and Dumb Asylum. He deeded to Jefferson County land for a courthouse and jail. On June 13, 1821, the legislature officially recognized Elyton as the permanent seat of justice for Jefferson County. This grant of Federal lands in Alabama to a private institution in Connecticut was a unique departure from all former grants. See letter, Lila Mae Chapman to W. E. Henley, June 22, 1940 (in Southern Collection, Birmingham, Alabama, Public Library), and W. Stanley Hoole (ed.), "Elyton, Alabama, and the Connecticut Asylum: The Letters of William H. Ely, 1820-1821," *Alabama Review,* III, 36-39 (January, 1950).

38 Colton's 1856 Alabama map shows clearly the East-West and North-South roads crossing at Elyton. The Huntsville Road, a part of the Great Tennessee Trail, came south from Nashville to Huntsville, Elyton, Tuscaloosa, and Mobile. The oldest road to enter Jones Valley, it was the main connecting link between North and South Alabama and an immigration trail for pioneers. At a later date, the Huntsville Road forked as it entered Jones Valley: the main prong passed through Roebuck and Elyton to Tuscaloosa; the other prong, called by Duffee the back road to Tuscaloosa, bore left and went by Green's and Jonesborough, rejoining the main prong before entering Tuscaloosa. In present day Birmingham, Tuscaloosa Avenue in West End, Vanderbilt Road in North Birmingham, as well as a few blocks still known as the Huntsville Road, mark the route of this once important thoroughfare. Also leading south was the road to Montgomery via Montevallo and Selma. The Montevallo Road left Jones Valley through Grace's Gap, proceeded by Oxmoor, Hale's Spring on Shades Mountain, down the present Montgomery highway for a mile or so, then to Pelham and Montevallo. Travel from Georgia came via Rome and Cedartown to Elyton. The Georgia Road entered Jones Valley several miles east of Elyton and then formed a junction with the Huntsville Road. See notes 10 and 75.

39 A. C. Montgomery, in an address on Elyton to the Birmingham Historical Society, April 15, 1943, describes the increased activity in Elyton with the influx of labor (some of which was Chinese) used in the construction of the North and South Alabama Railroad. J. D. Anthony, *Life and Times* (Atlanta, 1869), pp. 177-178, relates the difficulty he had "in 1870 in calling the Elyton people to things

of a spiritual character . . . Sunday, alas, was no exception to the rule . . . The people all expected to be millionaires" as they thought Elyton was to be the location of the railroad crossing.

40*Southern Business Directory* . . . p. 19, lists the following general merchants in Elyton: J. Camp, Earle and Wright, S. Steele, W. A. Walker and Joseph R. Smith.

41 Jefferson County Deed Book No. 1 (July 4, 1820) locates the courthouse site by referring to the Big Spring: "About the Big Spring near the foot of the prairies, etc." Tuomey, *op. cit.*, p. 21, notes it as "a magnificent limestone spring." Later known as the Eubank Spring, it is now just north of the Juvenile Court Building.

42 "Free citizens" came into usage after the Civil War. The small independent farmers of Walker County who owned few slaves desired no part in the Civil War. Their delegate to the Secession Convention of 1861 voted against the Secession Ordinance and refused to sign it. With the outbreak of war, however, the citizens, with a few exceptions who moved North, cast their lot with the Confederacy. See John Martin Dombhart, *History of Walker County, Alabama* (Thornton, Ark., 1937), pp. 45-46.

43 The first courts in Jefferson County were held in 1821 in a log hut about three-fourths of a mile west of present Avondale Springs. After several terms there the seat of justice was moved for two terms to another log cabin at Carrollsville, located at present Powderly. Subsequently, William Ely's grant for a courthouse at Elyton resulted in a more permanent brick edifice there.

44 Rhoda Coleman Ellison, *A Checklist of Alabama Imprints, 1807-1870* (University, Alabama, 1946), p. 7, lists James M. Norment as editor of the *Jones Valley Times*, first newspaper published in Elyton in 1854. It was followed in 1855 by the *Central Alabamian*, published for one year by Dr. Joseph R. Smith and Bayliss Grace, and subsequently for three years by Moses B. Lancaster. It was then bought by John Cantley of Tuscaloosa, who changed the name to the Elyton *Herald* and sold it to Henry A. Hale about 1865. The Elyton *Sun* was the last paper published in Elyton, about 1870. The same Washington hand press was used by all of these weekly papers. Robert H. Henley, first mayor of Birmingham, published the first paper there in 1871, the Birmingham *Sun*. In 1872 he sold it to Thomas McLaughlin and L. H. Matthews. Contrary to Duffee, no source consulted indicates that the *Jefferson Independent* was published in Elyton. The *Iron Age*, which succeeded the *Jefferson Independent* in 1874, became the first successful paper in the county. Charles Erastus (Ras) Cantley, brother of John Cantley, was the business manager. See John W. DuBose (ed), *Jefferson County and Birmingham, Alabama* (Birmingham, 1887), pp. 196-197.

45 Rutledge, *op. cit.*, p. 29, bounds the Elyton Precinct (1860) as follows: Shades Mountain west to Grace's Gap, northwest to present Pratt City, east to present East Birmingham, and southeast to Shades Mountain. This includes present communities of Green Springs, Ensley, Smithfield, Pratt City, Thomas, Avondale, and Birmingham.

46 As early as 1850 St. John's Parish, Elyton, was organized, due to the efforts of two sisters, Mrs. Nathaniel Hawkins and Mrs. Mortimer Jordan, who had come to teach school "in the wilderness of Jones Valley" with William Ely on one of his return visits to Elyton. Not until 1871 did the Parish have a church building. Then with funds and upon land given by the Nathaniel Hawkins family, St. John's Episcopal Church was erected. In 1873 St. John's became the Church of the Advent, Birmingham. Phillips A. Fitts served St. John's from 1871-1873, and the Church of the Advent from 1873-1875 (George M. Cruikshank, *A History of Birmingham and Its Environs*, Chicago, 1920, pp. 279-280).

47 *Jones Valley Times*, April 8, 1854, carried the following advertisement: "Strike while the Iron is *Hot!* Dr. J. R. Smith has yet on hand a few unimproved lots

in 'New Town', . . . just without the corporate limits of Elyton . . . a beautiful elevated situation, within half a mile of both the Male and Female Institute."

48 John W. DuBose (ed.), *Mineral Wealth of Birmingham* (Birmingham, 1885), pp. 183-184, concurs with Duffee in describing Smithfield "as the most important suburb of Birmingham." Today it is the location of a Negro Federal Housing Project.

49 "Col. W. S. Earnest has on Shades Mountain, a vineyard of scuppernong grapes of 5 acres. . . . There is no part of the country that offers such rare inducements for a colony to engage in the cultivation of the grape." *(South* [New York], April 5, 1873).

50 William P. Barker's map of the City of Birmingham, Alabama [1872] shows the North and South Alabama and Chattanooga Railroads meeting at 14th Street and running between and parallel to 1st Avenue North and 1st Avenue South to 26th Street.

51 In the *Jones Valley Times,* May 13, 1854, "A Chapter in the Early History of Jones's Valley" states that John Jones, the first white settler of the valley, erected a shanty on the west side of the road above Jonesboro. "Between the time of his arrival and May . . . some fourteen others . . . from Giles County, Tennessee, arrived . . . and located on lands now owned by O. W. Wood, Esq., [present Woodlawn], six miles above Elyton on the Georgia road. Joseph Nations, Nat Nations, James Nations, Joel Raburn, Perry Raborn, Thomas York, Jonathan York, Sr. and Jr., David Brown and four others . . . were joined [in May] by Williamson Hawkins [who] . . . brought a bag of meal and two middlings of bacon. [They] lived mostly on milk and butter, . . . made good corn the first year, . . . went back to Tennessee and moved out their families in the fall."

52 The Ruhama Baptist Church was constituted March 27, 1819 by Hosea Holcombe. The school later known as Baker's Academy was not founded until 1859 by the Reverend Jacob H. Baker.

53 Edmond Wood came to this locality in 1824. The first post office of the colony was first called Rockville, then Wood Station. In 1886 the settlement was officially named Woodlawn for the home of Edmond's son, Obadiah Washington Wood. See Brown and Nabers, *op. cit.,* V, 186 (July, 1952).

54 This community was known as Oak Grove until about 1885 when it was named Huffman for postmaster R. W. Huffman.

55 *Jones Valley Times* carries an article, November 3, 1854, entitled "Silver Billy." According to this report, William Reed outmaneuvered the land speculators at the Tuscaloosa land sale, 1820, by literally sitting on a coffin filled with silver.

56 "On Monday last a drove of over a hundred mules past thro' [Elyton] on their way to Selma and Montgomery from Kentucky" *(ibid.,* September 7, 1854). Four droves of hogs were noted by the same paper on November 30.

57 Enon Church was admitted to membership in the Baptist Cahawba Association in 1823 (Hosea Holcombe, *A History of the Rise and Progress of the Baptists of Alabama,* Philadelphia, 1840, p. 193).

58 This cave was described as a "newly discovered cave" in the *Jones Valley Times,* November 10, 1854. Called Cedar Mountain Cave, it was located twenty miles above Elyton, one mile west of the Springville Road, 100 yards above the base of Cedar Mountain. The inside of the cave consisted of "various windings and apartments" under a "solid arch of limestone" 100 to 200 feet above. In 1952 the editors visited this cave, now known as Crystal Cavern.

59 *Appleton's Cyclopedia of American Biography* (New York, 1888), II, 247, states that Mary Gordon Duffee wrote a "Guide to the Mammoth Cave, Kentucky" and

guide books to various interesting places along the southern railways. *A Bibliography of Mammoth Cave*, compiled in 1924 by Willard R. Jielson, geologist of the State of Kentucky, lists an anonymous pamphlet, *L. & N. R.R. Subterranean Wonders*, which the editors have seen in the New York Public Library and believe that Duffee wrote.

60 Site of Rutledge Springs, now better known as Dolomite for Woodward Iron Company quarry opened in 1882.

61 Named for Cape Smith's fellow soldier, Toadvine of Georgia, who came to Smith's aid in an argument with another prisoner when they were both imprisoned by the United States Army at Rock Island during the Civil War (Brown and Nabers, *op. cit.*, v, 188-189, July, 1952).

62 *Jones Valley Times*, July 1, 1854, states: "We also understand that the great Lead mine on the Warrior River had at last been discovered." Walter B. Jones, "Index to the Mineral Resources of Alabama," Alabama Geological Survey *Bulletin 28*, (University, Alabama, 1926), p. 181, notes, "There is not a county in Alabama where there is not a tradition of a *lead mine*, said to have been worked by the Indians or early settlers. . . . "

63 "By 1852 Hagood's Crossroads had become Mt. Pinson, so named by horse-traders and jockeys from Pinson, Tennessee, who camped at the Crossroads with droves of mules and horses headed for Tuscaloosa and cotton plantations farther south" (Brown and Nabers, *op. cit.*, V, 187, July, 1952).

64 "There were few taverns in the newly settled communities, but almost all the farmers who live near the road will take in strangers and travelers, giving them what is called "dry entertainment; that is, board and lodging but without any spiritous liquors" (from a contemporary account quoted in Randle Bond Truett, *Trade and Travel around the Southern Appalachians before 1830*, Chapel Hill, 1935, p. 99).

65 The editors believe that Duffee refers to Silver Lake which is shown on the U. S. Geological Survey Map, 1904-1905, to be about three-fourths of a mile from Mt. Pinson.

66 David Hanby first came to the Alabama Territory as a blacksmith with Jackson's troops at the personal request of Jackson. "As early as 1827 . . . David Hanby and his sons purchased land in Jefferson County, one and one-half miles west of Hagood's Crossroads. . . . In 1840, Hanby purchased some lands from Charles Loggins near the Blount County line. On this land there was coal in the bed of the Warrior River." (Ethel Armes, *Story of Coal and Iron in Alabama*, Cambridge, 1910, p. 48). Tuomey, *op. cit.*, p. 89, describes above coal bed thus: ". . . another seam of coal is found, 20 inches thick, and separated from the section above by a stratum of sandstone 15 feet in thickness. This is the only instance of anything like regular mining in this whole region, and the first attempt at reaching the coal by means of a shaft. Mr. Hanby is the proprietor, and is prospecting the work with as much energy as the force he can command will allow, where he has to begin with inexperienced hands."

67 Hanby operated several mills. "In 1827 . . . (he) erected a mill purposely for wheat. He procured good millstone for grinding, and good bolters. This mill (though in Jefferson County) is not many miles from the lower part of Blount County and the people of Blount, . . . carried their wheat to that mill." (Powell, *op. cit.*, p. 48).

68 "Mr. Hanby's account of his attempts at the introduction of Alabama coal into the Mobile market, would furnish an amusing chapter on the difficulty of directing any trade from its accustomed channels. The intelligent proprietors of the gas works in that city, however, were not slow to recognize its value as a material for the manufacture of gas. Much of what has heretofore been carried to market, under the name of coal, included everything that resembled it in color; but I know from observation, that those engaged in the business at present take every reasonable precaution to reject all impurities." See Michael Tuomey, *Second Biennial*

Report on the Geology of Alabama (Montgomery, 1858), p. 95n.
69 Joel C. DuBose gives an account of the first navigation of these shoals by flatboat in Armes, *op. cit.*, p. 54. These shoals are now Lock 17, Warrior System of Locks.
70 See Gosse, *op. cit.*, pp. 305-306 for other boatmen's songs.
71 Captain W. Felix Hanby, commander of Company C, commonly called Hanby's Company, was wounded at Shiloh but served through the Civil War. John F. Hanby, 3rd Lt., was killed at Shiloh. The other brothers were enlisted men. Hanby's Company was organized in the northern portion of Jefferson County, Alabama, in the spring of 1861. On being mustered into the Confederate service at Huntsville, it became a part of the Nineteenth Alabama Regiment, commanded by Colonel (afterwards Lt: General) Joseph Wheeler. See *Nineteenth Alabama Regiment, Roll and History of Company C* (N.p., 1904), pp. 1-3,7.
72 William Preston Johnston, *The Life of General Albert Sidney Johnston* (New York, 1879).
73 DuPont Thompson says that "Uncle Billy Nabers" told this story of David Hanby's death: "Old Man Hanby lived in a house above the falls on Turkey Creek. News of Wilson's Raiders came to the neighborhood, and all the people fled to the hills except Hanby, who was deaf and did not hear the warning. He saw the Raiders coming and made a dash for the woods but was overtaken and shot. The Federals then picked up the body and threw it over the fence into Hanby's own yard."
74 West, *op. cit.*, p. 287, states that at Cunningham's as early as 1818 the first sermon was preached, and the first log church was built in 1819.
75 General Jackson's military road into Alabama came from Fayetteville, Tennessee, to Huntsville, then to Ditto's Landing on the Tennessee River; thence down the eastern part of Alabama to Ten Island Shoals on the Coosa and to the mouth of the Coosa River. The "Old Huntsville Road" or the "Tennessee Road" coincided with General Jackson's road from Fayetteville to Huntsville, then veered west through Jones Valley to Tuscaloosa, probably along the route pursued by General Coffee in his military expedition into this section. See notes 10 and 37.
76 *Statistical View of the United States . . . Being a Compendium of the Seventh Census* (1850), states that on 51,921 acres of improved land in Jefferson County, only 2,040 bushels of wheat were raised annually as compared with 342,743 bushels of corn.
77 On October 22, 1813, General John Coffee reported from the "Indian Lands" to General Jackson: ". . . proceeded eight miles further, came to the main Black Warriors town abandoned by the Inhabitants . . . found some corn in the fields and some old corn in cribs, fresh fish of One or two Indians, and no other signs— got in the whole about 300 bushels corn, burnt their town or counsel house and about 50 other buildings—this town is supposed to be the principal one of the tribe and the lowest down the river, . . ." (John Spencer Bassett, ed., *Correspondence of Andrew Jackson*, Washington, 1926, I, 335). From his headquarters 24 miles south of Ditto's Landing, General Coffee wrote to his wife on October 24, 1813: "I have this moment arrived here from a rout into the Indian County of 10 days, have been to the Black Warrior Towns . . . and find them all deserted by the Indians, leaving their corn and some other plunder behind. I burnt 3 towns but never saw an Indian" ("Letters of General John Coffee to his Wife, 1813-1815," *Tennessee Historical Magazine,* II, 275, December, 1916).
78 The two incidents which Duffee quotes from David Crockett are both found in recent editions of his *Autobiography.* Duffee mentions in another sketch that George Goffe, onetime owner of Blount Springs, corresponded with David Crockett and at the death of Crockett, he draped the hotel in mourning.
79 On April 25, 1814, General Andrew Jackson wrote to John Armstrong from Fort Williams: "Tomorrow I detail 600 men under the command of Brigadier General Johnston to scour the Cahauba with instruction after dispersing any bodies of the enemy that may still manifest symptoms of histility, to unite with me at Ft. Deposit." (Spencer, ed., *op: cit.,* I, 508). On the War Department map of

General Jackson's Campaign to the Creek Indians, 1813-14, Tullavahajah or Mud-town is shown on the west bank of the Cahaba River with the notation, "**Burnt by Jackson May 1, 1814.**"

80 John W. Monette, *History of the Discovery and Settlement of the Valley of the Mississippi* (New York, 1846), II, 433, quotes from the Washington, Miss., *Republican*, December 13, 1815: The advanced pioneers from Tennessee, who had explored the country upon the source of the Black Warrior, "considered it 'the land of promise,' and they impatiently awaited the completion of the surveys of the United States, when they were ready to cover it with their tens of thousands." In 1815, however, there were only a few white squatters in Jefferson County.

81 An advertisement in the *Jones Valley Times*, April 22, 1854, from James A. Mudd's general store lists Bateman's Drops for sale.

82 The reference here is believed by the editors to be to Blount Springs.

83 T. P. Abernathy, *Formative Period in Alabama, 1815-1828* (Montgomery, 1922), has an excellent chapter on the public lands, pp. 50-56.

84 Huntsville land office served Jefferson County until May, 1820, when the Tuscaloosa land office opened and served the southern part of the county. Rutledge, *op. cit.*, p. 20, notes that between 1819-1829, 65,000 acres of public land in Jefferson County were entered with the land offices.

85 *U. S. Statutes at Large*, 16 Cong., 2 Sess., March 2, 1821 (Washington, 1846), p. 612.

86 The *U. S. Census* (1850) lists John L. Gill with two stagedriver sons among his many children, William, aged 34, and James D., aged 28.

87 In the 1850's James R. Powell, one of the founders of Birmingham, and Robert Jemison of Tuscaloosa, merged their stagecoach lines into the company of Jemison, Powell, and Ficklin, which operated on every pike and highway through north and central Alabama until the incoming of the railroads (Armes, *op. cit.*, p. 224-225).

88 Some coaches were fitted with a breast strap to help hold the passengers in their seats. The stagecoach lines cared little about the passengers' comfort since they were paid by the government to carry the mail (Truett, *op. cit.*, p. 134).

89 By 1834 the schedules were so well organized as to be printed in booklet form for the convenience of the patronage (Rutledge, *op. cit.*, p. 83).

90 *Ibid.*, pp. 25-26, states that the precincts in the hill country or western district of the county were the poorest. In 1850 less than half its heads of families did not own land, and only 8 families owned 2000 acres or more.

91 Minnie Clare Boyd, *Alabama in the Fifties* (New York, 1931), pp. 115-116, quotes this description of the Jacks almost in its entirety as "valuable for the social record of the period."

92 In 1850 Jefferson County had 2267 slaves to its white population of 6714. See *U. S. Census* (Seventh), 1850 [Original MSS Returns], Alabama, XII, 194. In 1850 80% of the working people in the county were farmers (Rutledge, *op. cit.*, p. 57).

93 The Selma, Rome & Dalton, the fourth Alabama railroad, was chartered in 1848 and completed to Montevallo before 1858 (Armes, *op. cit.*, pp. 38, 112).

94 The railroad was incorporated December 12, 1853 (Frank Y. Anderson, compiler, *Laws Relating to the Lands Formerly Owned by the Alabama and Chattanooga Railroad Company*, Birmingham, 1885, p. 21).

95 See note 3, above, *Alabama Review*, IX, 136 (April, 1956).

96 In 1868 J. C. Stanton and his brother, D. N. Stanton, of Boston, "backed by predatory bankers of the East," bribed the state legislature to accomplish state endorsement for railroad bonds. The dramatic story of the sustained hoax is told in A. B. Moore, "Railroad Building in Alabama During the Reconstruction Period," *Journal of Southern History*, I, 421-441 (November, 1935); William Elejius Martin, *Internal Improvements in Alabama* (Baltimore, 1902), pp. 70-84; and James F. Doster, *Alabama's First Railroad Commission, 1881-1885* (University, Ala., 1949). The name was changed to Alabama Great Southern in 1877, when the railroad

was reorganized in the hands of English capital. See Allen J. Going, "The Establishment of the Alabama Railroad Commission," *Journal of Southern History*, XII, 3 (August, 1946).

97 In J. C. Stanton's *Statement of the Building of the Alabama and Chattanooga Railroad* (Chattanooga, 1878) the Elyton depot was listed in the May 15, 1871 inventory at $3500; a small depot at Jonesboro, $300; and a depot at Trussville, $2000.

98 Rutledge, *op. cit.*, pp. 59, 63, 71-72, lists for Jefferson County 25 grist mills in 1840; more than a dozen cotton gins in 1860; 4 tanneries in 1840; and 15 blacksmiths in 1850.

99 See above, *Alabama Review*, IX, 138 -(April, 1956).

100 A young unknown engineer, John T. Milner, was appointed by Governor Moore and was offered $10,000 to make the survey for the railroad. It was substantially through his efforts and enthusiasm that the road was eventually completed and Jefferson County's minerals developed (see Armes, *op. cit.*, pp. 109-120).

101 Milner, John T. *Report to the Governor of Alabama on the Alabama Central Railroad* (Montgomery, 1859), p. 112. Milner recommended Decatur as the northern terminus and Selma as the southern, because the Selma, Rome & Dalton Railroad was completed between Selma and Montevallo.

102 "A decade or more before the Civil War Duffee purchased the resort hotel at Blount Springs . . . and operated it successfully until 1869." See Brown and Nabers, *op. cit.*, *Alabama Review*, VI, 244 (October, 1953).

103 In 1860 the Alabama legislature adopted Milner's recommendations and granted a loan of $663,135 if the line were graded in five years (Armes, *op. cit.*, p. 121).

104 Frank Gilmer, president and majority stockholder of the Alabama Central, changed the terminus from Montevallo to Calera *(ibid.,* p. 123).

105 Frank Gilmer and John T. Milner went to Richmond to solicit financial aid from the Confederate Government, which agreed to help them extend the South & North as far as Grace's Gap. Subsequently, they organized the Red Mountain Iron & Coal Company, which with government aid built the furnace at Oxmoor, Shades Valley, near Grace's Gap. It went into blast in 1863. The output from Oxmoor was hauled to Selma on one wood-burning locomotive, the "Willis J. Milner" *(ibid.,* pp. 161-164).

106 Armes (p. 186) gives a complete list of blast furnaces and rolling mills in and near Jefferson County at the time of the Civil War. Jefferson County: Red Mountain Iron Works at Oxmoor, Cahaba Iron Works at Irondale; Tuscaloosa County: Roupes Valley Iron Works (Tannehill); Bibb County: Bibb Furnace at Brierfield, Little Cahaba Iron Works · at Brighthope, Brierfield Rolling Mill; Shelby County: Shelby Iron Works, Helena Rolling Mill, Shelby Rolling Mill.

107 At the beginning of the Civil War Tate was president of the Memphis & Charleston, the most important railroad in the state. In 1869 he agreed to complete the South & North from Montgomery to Decatur and equip it by April, 1871 *(ibid.,* pp. 217-218, 247).

108 The dramatic circumstances surrounding Tate's selling his contract to the L. & N. for $75,000 are told in *ibid.,* pp. 247-249.

109 Duffee omits discussion of Frank Gilmer, the man most responsible with Milner's help, both before the war and afterwards for promoting the South & North *(ibid.,* pp. 121-123, 215-217, 244-249).

110 Other charter members of the Elyton Land Company were Sam Tate, Campbell Wallace, Bolling Hall, J. N. Gilmer, Robert N. Greene, W. F. Nabers, and John T. Milner *(ibid.,* p. 222).

111 For a full and authoritative biography see *Life of James R. Powell . . .* (Brooklyn, 1930) by his daughter, Mary Powell Crane. Mrs. Crane acknowledges her

indebtedness to Mary Gordon Duffee: "An account of some of James R. Powell's struggles and achievements, covering interesting incidents that occurred during the twenty-five years of his stagecoach operations, is related in an unpublished manuscript by Mary Gordon Duffee. In 1881 she submitted this manuscript to Col. Powell for his approval and correction, but he never returned it to her. . . . The manuscript came to my mother's possession in November, 1882, when visiting on the Mississippi plantation. While cleaning his desk and assorting his papers, she found Miss Duffee's manuscript entitled 'The Life of the Honorable James R. Powell, Founder of Birmingham, Alabama.' . . . He [Powell] said that it was in the main correct as to facts, but he did not care for the exaggerated eulogy she bestowed upon him. . . . He gave it to my mother. The manuscript is in my possession, and I am indebted to it for much of the information found in this book" (pp. 48-49).

112 For Powell's stage interests in Jefferson County and vicinity *see* note 87, above, *Alabama Review*, IX, 283 (October, 1956).

"n" following page number refers to footnote

Circus, 29

Civil War (see also Wilson's Raiders), 2, 5-7, 10-11, 14, 25, 26, 29, 35, 43, 67-69:
Confederate Soldiers, 31, 40, 48-49, 75
Furnaces, 89n
Nineteenth Alabama Regiment, 44, 48, 87n
Twenty-eighth Alabama Regiment, 20, 22, 81n

Click, John, 50

Clift, George W., 43, 57, 58

Coal and Coal Mining, 1, 4-5, 12, 16, 17, 23, 37, 40, 42, 45-49, 54, 57, 64-65, 70, 77, 78n, 86n

Coalburg, 36

Cochran, John, 26

Cochran, William, 26

Cochrane, William, 35

Cochrane, Sophia Holland, 35

Coffee, Gen. John, 50-52, 87n

Confederacy, 67, 75, 76

Cook's Ferry, 53

Cotton, 19, 29, 63, 64, 65

Creeks:
Crooked, 57, 58
Cunningham's, 17
Five Mile, 17, 50, 58
Possum Creek, 43
Turkey, 17, 46, 50, 55
Valley, 17, 26, 31, 38, 50
Village, 17, 23, 28, 46, 61

Crocker, Jackson, 23

Crockett, David, 51-53, 87n

Cunningham, Elijah, 19

Cunningham, James, 39, 49, 53, 87n

D

Davis, Dr. Daniel, 15, 20

Davis, Jefferson, 75

Decatur, 31, 65, 74

Ditto's Landing, 16, 52

DuBose, John Witherspoon, 9

Duffee, Ella, 10

Duffee, Mary Gordon, 1-11, 78n, 79n

Duffee, Matthew, 2, 66, 78n, 81n, 82n, 89n

Duffee's Mountain, 8, 9, 11, 18

E

Earle, Paul H., 37

Earle, Dr. Samuel S., 37

Earnest, William, 38, 85n

Ely, William, 31, 83n

Elyton, 2, 5, 7, 11, 12, 15, 26, 28, 31-38, 39, 40, 53, 55, 61, 63, 64, 66, 67, 69, 74, 83n:
Churches, 35
Courthouse, 14, 34, 84n
Newspapers, 35, 84n
Pioneers, 36-38
Stores, 34, 36, 84n
Tavern, 34

Elyton Land Company, 71, 89n

Elyton Spring, 23, 28, 34, 35

F

Fink, Albert, 70

Fitts, Rev. Phillip, 35

Flowers, 25

Fowler, John, 18

Friel, Thomas, 42

Friley, Caleb, 16

Frog Level, 83n

Fruit Culture, 18-19, 38, 58, 65

Furnaces, 89n:
Alice, 39
Brierfield, 6, 67, 69
Oxmoor, 6, 67-69
Round Mountain, 14
Roupe Valley Iron Works, 14
Shelby, 67
Tannehill, 5, 14
Woodward, 53

G

Gadsden, 19, 74
Gill, Jack, 55
Gill, Jim, 55
Gilmer, Frank, 1, 89n
Gilmer, J. N., 89n
Goffe, George, 87n
Goffe House, 2
Grace, Bayliss Earle, 69, 81n
Grace's Gap, 17, 70, 81n
Greene, George L., 44
Greene, Robert N., 44, 89n
Grimes, Billy, 58
Grimes Spring, 49
Guntersville, 19, 74
Gunter's Landing, 50

H

Hagood Mountain, 45
Hagood's Crossroads, 45, 49, 86n
Hall, Bolling, 89n
Hall, Samuel, 39
Hanby, David, 4, 45, 46, 49, 50, 78n, 86n, 87n
Hanby, Felix, 46, 49
Hanby, Jesse, 48
Hanby, John, 48, 49
Hanby, Milton, 48, 49
Hardeman, Tyler, 39
Harris, John, 58
Harrison, James, 26
Harrison, John, 26
Hawkins, David, 24
Hawkins, James, 41
Hawkins, Mrs. Nathaniel, 84n
Hawkins, Williamson, 16, 28, 29, 30, 35, 39, 83n, 85n
Hawkins' Spring, 23, 82n
Hearn, Rev. Ebenezer, 49
Helena, 43, 67
Henley, John, 26
Henry, John, 46
Hewitt, James W., 46

Hickman, Joseph, 25, 34, 39
Hillman, 50
Hillman, Daniel, 14
Hudson, Richard, 41, 42
Huntsville, 53, 55
Hurricane Creek, 12

I

Indians, 16, 22, 23, 25, 35, 39, 41, 43, 49, 50, 51-52, 53, 54:
Camps and Towns, 16, 23, 51, 52, 57, 81n, 87n
Legends, 44, 52
Mounds, 23, 81-82n
Trade, 16, 23
Trails, 16, 31, 44, 52, 61, 81n
Tribes, 16, 43, 50, 52, 54
Wars, 16, 39, 50-52
Iron and Iron Making (see also Furnaces), 1, 4, 5, 14, 16-17, 23, 31, 64-67, 68, 70, 75, 76, 80n, 81n

J

Jackson, Gen. Andrew, 49, 50-51, 52, 87n
James, Thomas, 53
Jasper, 31
Jacks, James, 58
Jefferson County, 6, 7, 18, 20, 23, 26, 31, 34, 41, 49, 50, 55
Jemison, Robert, 88n
Jemison Station, 67
Johnston, Gen. Albert Sidney, 49
Johnston, Isaac, 52
Jones, Andrew, 16
Jones, Dr. Andrew, 16
Jones, Jeremiah, 16, 53
Jones, John, 16, 22, 53, 85n
Jones, Billy, 55
Jonesboro, 15, 18, 19, 20, 22, 23, 24, 26, 30, 31, 35, 38, 41, 43, 81n

O

Oak Grove, 40
Owen, Thomas M., 4
Owen, Marie Bankhead, 9
Oxmoor, 6, 67-69

P

Peck, Judge, 37
Perkins, William, 53
Point, Maggie and Isaac, 11
Possum Valley, 20, 34, 43, 81n
Powell, Addison, 73
Powell, James R., 7, 37, 38, 71-77,
88n
Powers, Ira, 45
Powers, John, 36, 45
Prude, Mary, 14
Prude, William, 16
Pullin, William, 25

R

Railroads, 43, 63-69, 88-89n:
Alabama and Chattanooga, 64
Alabama Central, 1, 65
Alabama Great Southern, 12,
39, 64
Louisville and Nashville, 8, 70
Northeast and Southwest, 7, 12,
63-64, 80n
Selma, Rome and Dalton, 44, 63
South and North, 7, 39, 43, 50,
64-69, 71, 80n, 83n, 85n, 88n,
89n
Red Mountain, 1, 4, 16, 67, 71
Reed, William, 40
Revis, Draper, 53
Riley, Sallie, 38
Rivers:
Alabama, 52, 65
Cahaba, 16, 40, 41, 52, 61
Coosa, 19
Sipsey, 51

Tennessee, 16, 31, 50, 52
Warrior, 4, 16, 17, 19, 23, 31,
44, 49, 51, 61, 63
Roads, 8, 31:
Eastern Valley, 22
Federal, 87n
Georgia (Old Georgy Road),
39, 83n
Huntsville, 2, 16, 23, 26, 39, 41,
42, 44, 45, 52, 53, 57, 83n
Montevallo, 36, 83n
Plank, 12, 80n
Tuscaloosa, 19, 25
Roebuck, George James and Ann,
41
Roebuck's, 2, 20, 23, 39, 42, 43, 44
Roebuck Spring, 41
Roupe, William, 16
Roupe's, 15
Roupe's Creek, 14
Roupe's Valley, 16, 54
Ruhama, 25, 39, 40
Rutledge Springs, 43
Rutledge, James, 43

S

Salem, 26
Sand Mountain, 65, 70
Schools, 26-28, 82-83n:
Carrollsville, 24-26
Elyton, 26, 82n
Jonesboro, 26
Pleasant Hill Academy, 22-23,
81n
Ruhama, 39-40
Salem, 26
Selma, 31, 43, 50, 63, 68
Shades Creek, 40, 61
Shades Mountain, 22, 38
Shades Valley, 61
"Silver Billy", 40, 85n
Silver Mine, 23
Simmons, Jonathan, 53

Sketches of Alabama, 2-4, 7, 8, 9, 78n, 79n, 80n

Slaves and Slavery, 20-22, 29-30, 37, 43, 58, 64, 83n

Smith, E. Cape, 43

Smith, John, 38

Smith, Dr. Joseph R., 26, 28, 34, 36, 38, 61, 84-85n

Smith, Oliver M., 43

Smith, William D., 26

Songs, 48, 79n

Spencer, Leonard, 29

Springville, 40

Squaw Shoals, 5, 46

Steele, Jonathan, 46

Steele, Judge Wilson Sylvester, 37

Stony Lonesome, 24, 26, 42, 53

Stroup, Moses, 6, 14, 69

T

Talladega, 74

Tannehill, Ninean, 14

Tarrant, Benjamin, 53

Tarrant, James, Sr., 20

Tarrant, Rev. James, 36

Tarrant, Samuel A., 20, 81n

Tate, Sam, 89n

Taverns, 1, 34, 57, 86n

Thomas, John, 22

Thomas, M. C., 15

Thomas, William, 15

Thompson, James, 16

Toadvine, 43

Transportation (see also Railroads, Roads), 2, 31, 75:
Flatboat Travel, 5, 19, 46, 87n
Stage Travel, 12, 24, 31, 36,

55-57, 63, 74, 75, 88n
Wagon Travel, 12, 48, 63

Truss, Thomas K., 41

Truss, Warren, 40

Truss' Home Guards, 41

Trussville, 40, 41

Tuscaloosa, 1, 2, 4, 5, 7, 12, 14, 15, 19, 26, 31, 35, 46, 48, 50, 52, 55, 63, 64, 68, 83n

U

University of Alabama, 12, 35

V

Vann, James, 40

W

Walker, Richard, 36

Walker, William A., Sr., 34, 36

Wallace, Campbell, 89n

Warrior Station, 55

Washington House, 2

Wheeler, Gen. Joseph, 49

Wilson, Judge W. L., 40

Wilson's Raiders, 14, 20, 43, 49, 67-69, 80n

Wood, Edmond, 40, 85n

Worthington, B. P., 71

Worthington, Henry H., 73

Worthington, J. W., 10

Y

Young, Joe, 51

Designed by Karl Scott
Printed by Commercial Printing Company,
Birmingham, Alabama